'miserrimus' [by F.m. Reynolds]

"MISERRIMUS."

LONDON:
PRINTED BY W. WILCOCKSON, WHITEFRIARS.

"Miserrimus."

ON A GRAVESTONE IN WORCESTER CATHEDRAL
IS THIS EMPHATIC INSCRIPTION,

MISERRIMUS;

WITH NEITHER NAME NOR DATE, COMMENT NOR TEXT.

SECOND EDITION.

" La durée de nos passions ne depend pas plus de nous, que la
durée de notre vie."

" Plus on aime une maîtresse, et plus on est près de la haïr."

LONDON :

THOMAS HOOKHAM,

OLD BOND-STREET.

MDCCCXXXIII.

TO

WILLIAM GODWIN, ESQ.

THIS VOLUME

IS INSCRIBED,

AS A SINCERE, THOUGH TRIFLING, TOKEN

OF

REGARD AND ESTEEM.

ADVERTISEMENT

TO THE

FIRST EDITION.

THIS little volume was originally printed for private circulation; but, in consequence of circumstances of a simply individual nature, and therefore unworthy of record, it is now presented to the public in a new typographical form.

As, during the narrative, allusion is rarely made to the era, and to the character of the times, the reader is requested to bear in mind, that the principal events occurred in the reign of Charles the Second; when the

internal government of the country was so
lax, that in the remote and thinly peopled
provinces, the wealthy and the powerful
might have perpetrated, with little fear of
legal retribution, the wildest act of social
oppression and delinquency.   So long as his
more exalted subjects abstained from political indiscretions, neither the king nor his
cabinet cared to examine too closely into
their private enormities.

On a gravestone in Worcester Cathedral is
this emphatic inscription, *Miserrimus*.   No
name, date, symbol, text, or comment is
appended; nor any clue to the country,
station, or career of the individual thus un-
happily and terribly distinguished.   Whether
a clue has or has not been found, and

whether the following pages are a genuine or fictitious auto-biography, are questions which must be submitted to the solution of the reader ; who will, no doubt, decide according to the confidence or suspicion with which Nature has endowed him.

ADVERTISEMENT

SECOND EDITION.

It has been observed by a most respectable publication, that the hero of the following pages does not embody the idea which the inscription on the tombstone would naturally beget in the mind of a reflective person. The word *"Miserrimus,"* it is asserted, engenders feelings of charity and sympathy, and invests with a tender and plaintive interest the individual to whom it has been applied; whereas, the principal personage of this volume has been endowed with so fiery and villanous a character, that he fairly merits the designation of *Furiosissimus*.

The word "Miserrimus," attached by himself, or by another, to a *living* and guiltless person, would certainly invest him with a tender and plaintive interest; but, considered as an epitaph, it assumes a very different aspect, it no longer characterizes existing misfortune, but the memory of the dead. The greater the sufferings of a good man in this mortal state, the greater his happiness in escaping from it; only so long as he endures the ills of humanity is he "Most Wretched:" his bequest for his tombstone would be *Felicissimus*. No sorrow can extend beyond the grave, but that which originates in a life of sin.

These are the reasons which have led the author to *his* interpretation of this impressive epithet, and to the portraiture of his hero as a villain of the darkest die; but, not so consistently callous as to be incapable of experiencing the most heart-rending remorse.

The author never would have adopted this epitaph as the ground-work for a fiction, had he been aware that the name and career of the individual who selected it were known; but he received the first intimation of their publicity through the medium of the periodicals which reviewed his work. In them it was stated, that he was a conscientious priest, whose sufferings arose in his adherence to his religion. But, the exception does not constitute the rule: few virtuous men would be guilty of the eccentricity of stigmatizing their memories with the epithet of "Miserrimus."

The author's first knowledge of the existence of this epitaph originated in a conversation with Mr. Wordsworth; who afterwards wrote a sonnet upon it, which was published some five or six years ago in the "Keepsake." This avowal would have been made in the advertisement to the First Edition, but the author was then unwilling to appear in his own proper character.

An objection has been urged against the grammar of the title-page. It is averred that it is erroneous to declare that there is no " text " upon the tombstone; for " Miserrimus " is the text upon which a fiction of two hundred pages has been constructed. These censors forget that many of our English words possess various and discrepant significations; that the word *bull,* for instance, may denote " a blunder," a " papal letter," and the " male of black cattle;" and that " text " *may* mean a " scriptural quotation."

"MISERRIMUS."

On a gravestone in Worcester Cathedral is this in-scription—*Miserrimus;* with neither name nor date, comment nor text.

THE hand of the fiend was on me at my birth.

Even in extreme infancy I exhibited the utmost violence of character. I was frequently a prey to tempestuous bursts of passion, which intimidated the weak, and inspired the more reflecting with pain and disgust.

It were of little consequence to the interest of the fearful history which I purpose to re-late, were I to reveal the names and fortunes of my parents. Even, however, if they had possessed the celebrity of rank, honour, and station, been ennobled rogues with all the delusion of ancestral splendour and iniquity attached to them, I would not have attempted to have palliated my vices beneath the hereditary claim to flagitious indulgence. But, as they were honest and obscure, I will not drag them into infamous notoriety by declaring that they were so unhappy as to give birth to that most wretched being, who, under a name too celebrated, contrived, during a long series of years, to direct the attention of Europe to his talents, his successes, and his delinquencies.

The thoughtless are too prone to undervalue the claims of boyhood to intelligence and energy. To the adult's superficial view of the feelings and perceptions of youth may be attributed the after errors of many a wayward spirit. Had I been so fortunate as to have possessed parents who could have studied the depths of my character, and have availed themselves of their knowledge, I might not now have to recur to a life of unparalleled crime.

I was naturally crafty, and often in my earliest years have I gloried in the consciousness of successful deceit. Often have I listened to some inconsiderate confession while I appeared engrossed by my puerile amusements ; and often have I planned some intricate revenge while I have laughed with the individual I sought to injure. And, afterwards, in all the ecstasy of triumphant malevolence, I have said to myself, " They deem me inoffensive—a *boy* —a mere boy ; but the poison of the upas tree is within, and I will carry its desolation

C

into the homes of the happy, and their hearts
I will lay waste as with fire and sword."—How
little were those who superintended my education inclined to suppose that I could have
entertained such thoughts as these!

Let those interested in the instruction of
youth be assured that the passions of the boy
are as strong as, if not stronger than, those of
the man; though fortunately he has not the
same power of gratifying them, or their effects
would indeed be fearful.

Almost the earliest incident of which I have
now a recollection was a visit I was permitted
to make at the house of a school-fellow. We
lay in different beds in the same room. He
was a quiet, affectionate, kind boy, who by
his good-humour and endearing vivacity had
won the hearts of all who domesticated with

him. In the morning he asked me how I had slept? I replied, in a voice that howled with rage, and with the spirit of the demon looking out at my eyes, "I have remained awake the whole night, and I have cried through every minute of it, in order that I may be able to show a sick face to your father, and declare that you have tormented and beaten me."

This anecdote may appear frivolous, but it is too emphatically indicative of my character to be omitted.

We returned to school; and my antipathy to this boy increased to a fearful degree, simply, I believe, because, in spite of all my wiles, he was more popular than I. Oh, if there be on earth a passion which carries a hell into the bosom of its possessor, it is the hate which is the offspring of envy !

My detestation for my school-fellow eventually attained that height, and the insults and aggressions which I practised upon him were so ferocious, that, at last, even his mildness was turned into gall. He resented some provocation, I struck him, and we fought. Heart-broken as I now am, the rage and malice of that moment appear to me like a dream. I can scarcely imagine that this enervated, prostrated mind can ever have entertained passions so violent and so demoniac.

I fought with my spirit even more than with my body—my whole soul was in every blow ; but still I did not succeed. At last, I fell senseless on the grass, and my enemy remained the conqueror of his oppressor.

From that moment, the darkest feelings which can disgrace poor human nature took possession of my breast. I lived only in the expectation of revenge; and an opportunity for attaining it offered itself too soon. I was tyrannising over an unfortunate boy, who was weeping and writhing beneath my inflictions, when a violent blow suddenly felled me to the earth. I rose, and discovered that I had endured this indignity at the hand of the being I most loathed. He reproached me for my dastardly conduct, and then walked placidly and triumphantly away. I meditated for a moment; then crept stealthily after him, drew my knife from its sheath, and plunged it up to its handle in his back.

In his turn, he fell to the ground, and I stood over him, in thought, if not in deed, a murderer!

His wound, though a very severe one, having been pronounced not to endanger his life, his relatives and friends were content that my only punishment should be a dismissal from the school with every circumstance of ignominy. Accordingly, on one bright sunny day, when not a cloud interposed its friendly shade to obscure the expression of the emotion which malice, hatred, and shame begot on my distorted countenance, I was led to the principal entrance, and, amidst the execrations and revilings of my assembled school-fellows, and the reproofs and disgust of the officials, thrust through the old arch. Its iron gates closed

with a clash that vibrated to my very soul;
the entire crowd of spectators raised one
general acclamation of scorn and defiance,
and I walked on my course, solitary, dis-
honoured, and debased.

This detail of puerile incidents may, I repeat, appear frivolous ; but, as mine is rather
a history of passions and emotions than of
actions, I feel that I ought not to omit the
recapitulation of any feature that might tend
to convey a correct estimate of the general
tenor of my anomalous mind.

Anomalous indeed !—but in this possession
I am not singular. Anomaly enters into the
composition of us all; *impar sibi* is the bio-
graphy of every created being, and *I* have
proved no exception to the rule.

After my ignominious expulsion from school,

I returned to my parents. My father was an extensive landholder in a northern county, who himself farmed the estate which he inherited from a long line of respectable ancestry, and lived in the narrow circle of rural society, unknowing and unknown to the great world. With him I led an idle life, and flourished in body, if not in mind, until I grew into vigorous youth. At the age of eighteen, my fond father seeing that I manifested no repugnance to his occupation, and none more ambitious offering itself, at his instigation, I became a tiller of the land, and pursued my avocations at first with industry, and at last with interest. There is something in the tenor of this employment which is inimical to the strength of the evil passions; as the exposition to the air braces the body, the communion with nature softens the mind. The most innocent period of my life was the three first years which I devoted to agriculture.

For a long time, an estate that immediately adjoined the property which my father cultivated had been untenanted. It was of considerable extent, and, in addition to many acres of fine arable and pasture land, comprised a good house and park, gardens, wood, water, and all the ornamental features which a wealthy family could desire. It was in A.D. 1670, and on the very day on which I entered into my twenty-second year, this domain found a purchaser and an occupant. I heard of the event with apathy, for little did I then imagine its consequences.

A short time afterwards, I first encountered

her whom destiny had selected to be the instrument of my moral and physical, my worldly and eternal ruin. The morning was exquisitely beautiful; both earth and heaven smiled. It was the poet's month of May; and nature, animate and inanimate, held a universal jubilee. Listening to the carols of the birds, and watching the gambols of the deer, I was straying, in a happy state of animal enjoyment, along the banks of a lovely stream, when I heard the notes of a harp accompanying a female voice exquisitely melodious. To this hour the subject of that song haunts me; for, independently of the deep impression it then made, I had afterwards too fatal a reason for never forgetting it: it was the famous hymn to the Virgin, *Maria santissima, madre amata.* With all

the fervour of religion, and the beautiful in-
tonations of natural sensibility, conjoined to
the skill of a practised musician, the invisible
singer poured forth her heavenly strains.
Rooted to the spot under the influence of this
divine charm, I listened in an intensity of
sympathy and rapture, until I felt the warm
tears trickling down my cheek. Aroused by
this proof to the consciousness of a weakness
which I had never before experienced, and
which I deemed degrading, I cautiously proceeded in the direction of the sounds, and at
last discovered, though unseen by her, the
being who had so moved me.

Oh, God! if ever the spirit of an angel
abode on earth, it was incarnate in that girl!
So hallowed, and yet so brilliant was her
beauty, she seemed a personification of light!

Her bright eyes—her bright hair—her pure
skin—her perfect form—her upturned countenance, radiant with the devotion of her soul,
and the scarcely brighter sun which shone in
deceptive beams through the interstices of the
foliage, above, around, and upon her, all
combined to strengthen the illusion.

With a broken and a bleeding heart, and
as an act of expiation, willingly would I
compel myself to expatiate on the whole detail
of her charms, and summon before me, feature
by feature, the image of the being who
consecrated humanity; whose life was one
continued career of innocence, honour, and
happiness, until, like a demon, I swept across
her path, and blasted the peace of her un-
sullied heart. Willingly would I impose upon
myself any, and every, infliction; but this I

cannot, *dare* not endure. In the most emphatic sense of the term, she was *beautiful;* and here I abandon the theme.

We met: and we met again and again. It is not essential to the development, or to the interest of my narrative, to relate how the deeper tone of our intercourse began, or proceeded. Words, indeed, could but feebly express its progress; for every faculty was engaged more than that of language, in promoting it. We had not exchanged more than the most meanless phrases of formal intercourse, when a mutual, though scarcely conscious, intelligence was established. And yet she spoke, and spoke most eloquently; but her *eye* was the organ of her eloquence.

Her father, our new neighbour, did not disdain to visit, on terms of perfect equality,

our less pretending abode. He was a widower,
and possessed this only daughter, and a son,
an officer in the navy, who was then serving
on a foreign station. He was descended from
an ancient though not a noble family; he had
been a Member of the Commons, and the
political part he played during the Revolution,
rendered him no favourite with the existing
government. Though not remarkable for in-
tellectual energy, he was a mild, worthy man,
and a doting parent.

I had two sisters, artless, endearing girls,
who rapidly conceived an enthusiastic friendship for her, which she as speedily returned.
This intimacy induced a still closer union
between us; and in the park, in the glen, on
the lake, in the village church, in our respec-
tive homes, we repeatedly encountered. Tran-

scendently fond of the charms of nature, we used to pass hour after hour, roving beneath the open sky, inhaling the pure air by the side of the brook, or on the brow of the hill. Selecting the most beautiful spots for our resting-place, we would sit and while away many a happy morn and eve, in that delicious indolence which can only be felt by the healthful and the contented. Whilst my sisters supported a desultory conversation, in which she occasionally attempted to join, I gazed on her countenance with undisguised admiration, and lost myself in dreams of happiness without alloy. With the beautiful and graceful modesty of youth and innocence, in sweet confusion she would strive to appear unconscious of my scrutiny; but, ever and again, with the exultation, the happiness which a lover alone can know, I marked her emotion rise beneath her transparent skin, and crimson her whole face with one exquisite blush.

How accurate is the observation of La Bruyère :—" *Etre avec les gens qu'on aime, cela suffit ; rever, leur parler, ne leur parler point, penser à eux, penser à des choses plus indifferentes, mais auprès d'eux, tout est égal.*" To the truth of this passage all who have really loved can willingly testify. But how few *have* really loved ; how many millions are born without the power of entertaining this dangerous happiness.

In her presence, I rarely spoke ; my feelings were too strong for utterance. Intense passion is ever taciturn and contemplative ; yet how many women are won by vivacity and fluency of speech. They are amused; and insensibly they attach a value to the society of the individual who amuses them. They marry, and discover, when too late, that they have found a companion, but not a lover: that they are united to a head, but not to a heart. How well is this sentiment expressed in this pretty quatrain:—

> " Qui ne sent rien, parle à merveille ;
>   Doutes d'un amant rempli d'esprit ;
> C'est ton cœur, et non ton oreille,
>   Qui doit écouter ce qu'il dit."

Strange that I, who stand with my eyes opened on the grave, who have abjured the things of this world, should yet derive a morbid gratification from the discussion of this worldly theme. Yes, even in this moment, the ruling passion of a life can make

D

itself felt. Behold the nature of man; the littleness and inconsistency of his character adhere to him even in the hour of his death. It has been repeatedly observed, that an infinitely greater number of individuals terminate their lives by drowning, in the summer, than in the winter; the dread of the cold shock of the immersion possessing more influence over the minds of the fastidious wretches than the dread of the dread hereafter.

At this period a striking change occurred in my character. The effect of passion is to brutalize; but the effect of love is to elevate. The man who really adores, dares not even secretly transgress; he feels as though he were ever beneath the eye of his mistress. Hitherto I had been the slave of many a way-

ward and sensual caprice; but under the con-
secrating influence of her purity, a new and
better spirit grew within me. The coarseness
of man's nature forsook me, and an unknown
delicacy, a refinement, a fastidiousness of sentiment, arose in its place. I turned from my
former thoughts and reflections with disgust;
I loathed the vulgar levity which might
once have amused me; and the voice of
the libertine and the bacchanalian became
abominations in my ears.

There are many who imagine that they love.
Would they seek to learn whether their con-
jecture be well or ill founded,—let them ask
themselves if they desire to insult the object
of their attachment by either deed or word.
Should they hear a small still voice answer

in the affirmative, let them be assured that " the truth is not in them."

When we did not expatiate on our own feelings and anticipations, almost her only topic of discourse was her absent brother, of whom she was passionately fond. The affection which this ardent girl entertained for him, could scarce be conceived by a mind naturally less enthusiastic, or more subdued by worldly discipline. Romantic, gifted with a powerful imagination, and glowing with feeling, when she descanted on the qualities and excellencies of her brother, her speech rose into the highest order of eloquence. In those moments, with her flushed cheek and sparkling eye, her varying tone and animated gesture, she realized my youthful dream of the inspired Pythia of Delphi, revealing the oracle of her god; before, I need not add, the rude Thessalian had caused the young and the lovely to be superseded by the staid matron of fifty.

After my own heart was she formed; had I been endowed with the power of Prometheus, I could not have created a being that would have more perfectly embodied all my ideas of female excellence. All that she said, looked, and did, possessed a grace peculiarly her own. The wealthy and the gay are too often the apathetic and the unfeeling; engrossed in their narrow egotism, they are not even conscious that they possess not the power of sympathising in the welfare or the wo of others. But *she* was the child of sensibility, quick to joy, and quick to mourn; with a smile for the

vivacious, and a tear for the sorrowing.   Unlike the rigid, frigid woman of the world,
never did I see her in a state of passiveness;
always awake to the interest of the passing
scene, her life was one endless variety of
emotion.

Affectionately attached to her parent, her
reliance on him was boundless; whatever he
taught, she believed; the possibility of his
erring could never even have entered into
her imagination. I often dwelt with pleasure
on this trait in her character, and thought
that one who had been so fond a daughter
could never prove a heartless wife; and there
was, is, and ever will be, truth in this mode
of judgment. Learned, and skilled in all the
attainments and arts adapted to a female mind
and hand, she was wise without affectation,

or even the consciousness of her knowledge. Ignorant of the pride of birth, fortune, or station, she possessed, in its fullest extent, the pride of integrity, sincerity, and delicacy. Elegant, but not fastidious; lively, but not volatile; dignified, but not severe; refined, but not artificial; feminine, but not enervate; the daughter of field and plain, not of the sickly city, she could dance upon her native soil, with step as light, and limb as free, as Euphrosyne's, " when the merry bells ring round." Like Ariel, too, she could " climb the mountain," and could have " plunged the deep" as boldly, had the usages of her time and sex permitted her; for though timid as a fawn, and as graceful in her timidity, she possessed none of the idle apprehensions which oppress the languid mind and body of the pallid slave of the crowded town.

And yet she was no angel; she was that better thing—a lovely woman. She had failings—failings which originating in her very virtues, served only to enhance the power of her fascinations. She had all the softness, pliancy, and impetuous tenderness of her sex; yet she sometimes exhibited a masculine vigor of mind. Variable as an April day; the creature of impulse and passion, warm, generous, and affectionate, in a pre-eminent degree, I occasionally thought, or fancied, that her zeal might be hurried into rashness, her confidence into credulity, and her energy into obstinacy. But then, I remembered that the surface of our earth produces flowers and fruit, though many a volcano may lie sleeping beneath it; and I loved not her virtues the less, because they might cover a disposition to error, which time itself might never develop. But it is one of the strongest evidences of the traces of the original sin, and of the consequent imperfection of our state, that, that very quickness and excitability of amiable and virtuous feeling, which bestow on a woman her greatest charm, constitute her principal liability to temptation and folly. Whether I judged her correctly, the sequel will show.

Her brother was her frequent correspondent; and one fine summer morning, she came to me in the wood, joyously displaying the letter which announced his immediate return. I thought that I had never seen her looking so radiantly beautiful.

In spite of the intimate communion which
existed between us, I had not yet dared to
declare to her the sentiments with which she
inspired me. For though I may say that I
entertained the conviction that she did not
regard them unfavourably; for though, in
short, in moments when reason exerted her
sway, I even felt assured that she *loved* me;
yet never did I resolve to speak boldly of my
love, but a morbid sensitiveness intervened,
and filled me with doubt, hesitation, and suspicion. Thus, though her looks, her acts,
her deep emotions, sufficiently proclaimed it
to an uninterested observer, I never yet had
obtained from her that decisive avowal of her
passion, which could alone satisfy me.

Like all those who have ever loved intensely, I was the unconscious victim of the

awe which she excited in me. It were impossible to express, scarcely possible to conceive, the fear, the apprehension, and the agitation I have endured in her presence. She had attained that mastery over me, that ever when I first appeared before her after a separation, however brief, my whole frame quivered, and every muscle and every nerve were spasmodic with emotion. I felt a difficulty even when alone in uttering her name; there appeared to me a profanation in breathing it to the silence and solitude of night— and at this moment I *dare* not record it; but, like Mary and her Calais, it will be found after my death engraven on my heart.

During the interview to which I am now recurring, I made repeated efforts to induce the conversation which I so intensely desired.

I felt more and more deeply that she loved me, loved me devotedly; but when I sought to declare my own sentiments and demand the avowal of hers, my tongue cleaved to my mouth, and the unintelligible words died in disjointed syllables on my parched lips.

She left me, and I remained on the spot in a transport of passion, invoking curses on my weakness, all the violence of my nature again breaking forth in the bitterness of this fancied degradation. I then swore with many a deep imprecation that no earthly power should prevent me from repairing to her that evening, and obtaining from her the final and irrevocable interchange of vows.

In this determination I commenced my return to my home. I emerged into the high road at the foot of a rather steep hill, which

I was musingly and abstractedly ascending, when, at some little distance below me, a carriage stopped, and a gentleman alighted from it. Unconsciously I noticed this proceeding, but took no heed of the individual. Leisurely I continued my path, still absorbed in my irritation, when I became aware that footsteps were rapidly overtaking me. Turning round, I perceived almost at my side the stranger whom I had previously so imperfectly remarked. But how shall I express the emotions which assailed me, when, on a nearer scrutiny, I recognised in that stranger the foe of my youth, the object of my hatred, the cause of my crime!

He recollected me. All the demon began to stir within me. The aversion, rancour, and fury, which during so many years had been suppressed, not extirpated, awoke, in renewed vigour, dilated my frame, and flashed from my eyes. What were his first emotions on meeting me I know not; but, stimulated, perhaps, by my undisguised hostility, he quickly retorted with looks of scorn and defiance. We walked side by side for some moments, at each step slightly approaching nearer to the other. Neither spoke; but, wrapped in silence, and in our own dark thoughts, both appeared to be contemplating the act of violence, which neither knew how to commence. At length we came into personal collision.

He suddenly stopped; and, with a strong effort controlling his passion, in a stern voice, and with a stately gesture, exclaimed :—

" Pass on !—*We* are not fit companions.

The world is wide ; and east and west, north and south must be our relative course through life."

" What !" I cried, " you fear me !—Am I then a lion in your path?—I knew not that I was so terrible."

" A lion !" he repeated with a bitter sneer, and his dark eyes glowed with contempt ; " a lion?—yes—a *stuffed* one—stuffed with your own self-esteem. Know, redoutable man, that the most opposite causes will sometimes produce the same result. From the lion I might turn in fear ; but *you* I deem as a reptile in my path, and I turn from you in disgust !"

" Stay," I cried, gasping with the violence of my passion, " and hear my defiance, villain that I loathe,—villain that I curse,—villain that I will annihilate!"

"*Murderer!*" he shouted in a voice of thunder.

I raised my arm,—he caught it in his grasp, and held it extended in the air with an amazing strength. Without motion, without effort, with our muscles rigid and distended with the animosity and malignity of our hearts, we stood for some moments, mutually regarding the face of the other with the expression and feeling of hyenas.

At length, withdrawing my arm, I exclaimed, " Not blows, but *blood!*"

" Agreed," he replied; " ours is a feud which can only end with the life of one or both."

" When and where shall we meet ?"

" In yonder wood, to-morrow, at sun-rise."

" And the weapons ?"

" Pistol and sword; we will not want for tools to dig ourselves a grave."

" My hatred is such," I rejoined, " that I cannot extend to you the courtesies of social life, nor wear before you the mask of reserved politeness. I cannot say farewell to one whom I wish every ill. I leave you now, my *living*, loathed, and loathing foe ; when next we separate, I hope to leave you on the *red* grass !"

We parted; and I returned to arrange the business which this rencontre had carved out for me. I obtained the promise of a friend to attend me on the following morning ; and I completed some testamentary documents,

E

by which I bequeathed the whole of the little property I possessed to her. To her I then addressed every thought; and this train of reflection induced an enervation which made me tremble at the recollection of the risk I was about to incur. That danger, however, rendered me still more resolved to finally determine that evening the unreal doubts which had so long, and so unnecessarily, agitated me.

With the greatest impatience I awaited the arrival of the hour when we were accustomed to meet in the garden, if not by an acknowledged pre-arrangement, at least by a tacit convention. Never did time appear to travel more slowly; but at length the moment arrived, and I commenced my walk.

When I reached the spot, I found that she was already there. She heard my foot steps, and turning round, abruptly confronted me. I then saw that she was violently agitated; her face was flushed, and the traces of tears were in her eyes. I rushed forward to meet her. She receded. In overwhelming anxiety, with outstretched arms, I still advanced, but she still withdrew.

" In the name of heaven," I cried, " tell me, I beseech you, what has befallen you'?" but she returned no reply.

I caught her in my arms.

" Dearest ———," I exclaimed, addressing her by her name, and folding her to my bosom, " speak, I implore, conjure you— what is the cause of this affliction?"

She slightly attempted to extricate herself from my embrace, but answered not.

" Torture me not, my loved, and may I

not add, my *loving* one? I came here
stimulated by the pangs and doubts of two
long years to entreat you to assure me that
you reciprocated in my affection, and this is
the reception you yield me!—What has dis-
turbed you?—Who has aggrieved you?—
Name him, and by the heaven above, he shall
not escape an awful retribution, if on earth
there can be a man so base as voluntarily
to cause the tears to flow from such eyes as
these! Suffer me to hear your voice.—Oh,
God, how terrible is this silence!—Speak to
me, dear, adored one, in your own soft tones
—tell me that your grief is unfounded;
and, oh! tell me, tell me, that you will be
mine!"

" *Never!*" she exclaimed, with a mighty
voice, and a fearful emphasis.

I stood as though in a dream; my arms no longer retained the power of embracing her; they fell by my side, and she availed herself of her release to withdraw a few paces from me.

At length I awoke from my prostration, and the power of utterance returned.

"*Never!*" I repeated; " oh, M———, retract this dreadful resolution!"

"Retract!" she cried, with wild energy; " what! wed a *murderer*—a murderer in mind, if not in deed—the murderer of my dear, dear *brother!*" and she sobbed convulsively.

God of heaven! what were then my feelings!

" Go!" she exclaimed, with an enthusiasm that seemed almost supernatural; " go! I

hate you, I loathe you, I despise you! The
dream is fled, the delusion is dissolved, and I
see the heart of a tiger beneath the disguise
of a man. Go, fiend! I denounce you! the
stain of blood is on you—hence! with the
curse of a fond sister, and a deceived woman,
to wander like Cain over the face of the land,
abhorred and abhorring!"

Bowed to the earth, I remained before
her, during this torrent of inspired passion.
Powerfully then did remorse work within
me; mighty was the expanse which it then
comprised. The distant past recurred with a
fearful distinctness; and the present, and the
fancied future, lay open before me. I looked
into myself, and I saw the evil of my heart;
and I resolved to pluck it out. Had she
then but listened to my fervent protestations

of atonement and expiation; had she been softened by the agony of my self-reproaches, and the intensity of my self-debasement, and accepted the sincerest repentance that ever was offered by a contrite sinner, I might have lived to have been a wise and a good man, instead of the thing I am. Oh, why did not heaven in that moment inspire her with its own beautiful precept, " There is more joy over one sinner that repenteth, than over ninety-nine just persons who need no repentance?" But the power of the fiend prevailed; she was inexorable; and I was lost.

" Treasure not," she exclaimed, " one hope, one little hope, in the corner of your corrupt heart. Between you and me fate has placed a gulf impassable. Your crimes have more

than extirpated my affection; they have en-
grafted aversion in its place."

Still I implored.

" Begone!" she cried: " or stay, and hear
me swear never again to entertain for you
any feeling but that of unmitigated hatred
and contempt!"

Hell entered into my heart, and fury
flashed from my eyes.

" Woman!" I exclaimed, with all the ferocity of insanity, " urge me not too far, or
by the heaven above, you shall live to learn
that I *can* be a murderer!" and I ground my
teeth, and beat the earth, in the paroxysm of
my desperation.

She trembled beneath my violence; the
colour fled from her cheeks, and the tears

gushed from her eyes, as she turned on me
a look of imploring anguish. I could not
resist this pathetic appeal; and my passion
immediately flowed in another channel.

" Curses on my cruelty !" I cried; " but
had I loved you less, I had been more for-
bearing. Now listen to me, while once more,
and for the last time, I implore your mercy ;
reflect, then, before you reply. Punish me
not for the crime of my youth; forgive me,
and the rest of my days shall be passed in
expiating it. Consider well my intreaty—
my life, my salvation, are dependent on your
decision. Answer not, deny me not rashly.
—Oh, God! gift me with the powers of per-
suasion, inspire me with the words of conviction, and every future hour shall be devoted to thy honour and service.——Turn

not away; let me gaze on your face, while on my knees I *pray*, for your own sake, for your brother's sake, reject not my contrition; but pardon, pardon, pardon!" and I lay on the earth before her.

Intense seemed the stillness around; and her low and sweetly musical tones sounded with an awful distinctness in my ears, as she deliberately, firmly, and solemnly replied,

" Never! never will I unite my fate to yours!"

" Devil" I cried, starting to my feet, " fly, and fly quickly! fly, ere I tear from your breast your false heart! Yet stay—stay, I command you, and hear me first retort your hatred: I hurl it in your teeth, proud, scornful, unfeeling, vindictive woman!—I defy thee, I hate thee, and I despise thee!—Now

listen; mark me, and forget not, I have fore-
warned you : whatever portion of life may
remain to me, I devote to evil—evil to thee
and thine! I tear thee from my heart, and I
sicken with disgust that such a silly, worthless
toy should ever have possessed it!—Oh that
I had words to make thee writhe as I desire,
thou fickle, loathsome thing!"

With an effort of almost superhuman self-
control, I watched her until she had dis-
appeared; and then, rushing into the wood,
I abandoned myself to the madness of my
despair. I tossed my arms in the air, in unholy
defiance of Heaven, and, in the strength of
my wickedness, blasphemously invoked and
dared the divine interposition ; then, casting
myself on the earth, I dug its flinty face with
my distended fingers, till, jagged and muti-

lated, even in the extremity of my agony I became conscious of their wounds. Goaded into additional fury by this corporeal smart, I rose with a hoarse shriek of passion, and, in a paroxysm of desperation, like a maddened bull, hurled myself against the solid timber of a mighty oak. I felt the sharp and gnarled points enter my brain; a torrent of blood blinded my eyes; a fearful sensation subdued me, and I sank on the earth in utter insensibility.

When I recovered my senses, the darkness of night was around: I gazed on the sky, but neither moon nor stars were there; all was wrapped in a pitchy darkness. The heavy dews which had fallen on me, and the loss of blood which I had sustained, had induced a stiffness in my limbs which at first rendered me incapable of all motion. At length, after many efforts, and infinite bodily torture, I succeeded in rising, and again looked around me in much anxiety, for I knew not how far the night was advanced. Having, however, somewhat re-assured myself, by observing no trace of day, I slowly commenced my painful return.

When I arrived at my home, I found, to my great relief, that midnight was scarcely passed. Several hours, therefore, must elapse before the rencontre of the following morning; hours most welcome, for never did exhausted nature more require repose than mine at that moment.

I slumbered uneasily until the first break of dawn, and then arose, but slightly refreshed. My wounds and bruises were still rigid and painful, and I felt heavy in mind and in body. But, when I regarded myself in my mirror by the fitful light of a flickering taper, never shall I forget the transport of rage with which I was seized. Though never a vain man, for my temperament was far too fiery to be ruled by the base passion of vanity, yet I attached that value to personal beauty which is the offspring of a desire to please those whom we love. Not, therefore, without gratification have I been conscious that I possessed a manly form and harmonious features.

But how shall I describe the image which now met my view?—*Hideousness* is a word far too feeble to represent it. My head was swoln to a fearful size; my eyes were starting from their sockets; a large and frightful gash divided my forehead; and my face and hair were incrusted with coagulated blood. Yet it was not this distortion, but the consciousness of the *cause* of it, which so madly exasperated me. I thought not on the loss of personal comeliness; but it was the association, the vivid retrospect which that loss excited, that made me call down curses on the head of the woman I had so recently adored.

All existence then seemed to me to be concentrated in one single word, *revenge*. Writhing under the intensity of this feeling, thirsting for another's blood to atone for the loss of my own, I repaired to the appointed spot. My friend had already arrived, and, after a few moments, my adversary and his second approached. In the misty and uncer-

tain morning light, he did not observe the
change, in my appearance, until we were
almost in contact. He started, and evidently
did not recognise in the monster before him,
the foe of his youth and of his manhood.
He gazed around him as though he expected
an explanation from the parties present, or
the arrival of a third person; when I exclaimed,

"Turn, fool! and see before you the man
who loves your company so well, he would
cheerfully die the death of Samson, and
immolate himself, rather than allow the Phi-
listine of his wrath and his abomination to
survive this hour of atonement!—*Now* do
you know me?"

"I do," he cried; "less by your avowal,

—for truth is a stranger to your heart and to your tongue—than by the malice of your sentiments."

" Believe me," I retorted, " I seek that my actions should not disgrace my words. See —the mist is before the sun; it is frail and transient: but, by the heaven that hears me, I swear, it shall be more enduring than one of us! *Both*, perhaps, may never again look on a cloudless sky.—And yet, I could almost rejoice to escape the doom I would bring on you; for I would rather endure the curse of existence, than share with you, even in that last best blessing—the grave!"

" Strange and unfathomable being," he impressively rejoined, " I gaze on you with wonder and with awe.—Are you above, or below, our mortal nature? for, surely so vast a wickedness cannot be of earth."

" I excite your wonder and your awe! What! can this external frame, this husk of the passions, so powerfully impress you? Oh that I could illumine my heart before you; *then*, indeed, you might quail!—Yes, look upon me well—you do not wrong me,—I *have* discarded the sympathies of my race:— and here I stand, a very reckless, a very desolate, and a very desperate man, possessed of no immortal, and of only one earthly hope, —that of spilling your blood."

" Consistent fiend!" he passionately exclaimed, " cannot you even here, on this spot, with the grave opening before you, entertain one human feeling?"

" Yes; I could be inspired with that of Mezentius, when he tied face to face the living and the dead; and could love to see you bound to your sister's corpse, only that then, *she* would be beyond my farther vengeance !"

Will it be believed that, even in the very act of expressing this odious wish, I was conscious that I still loved her whose destruction was the object of it?—Yet such was my inmost feeling, for such is mortal consistency !

But, resolved as I am to endure the pang of representing my character minutely and faithfully, without the slightest concealment or mitigation of its iniquitous features, yet I need not farther pursue this offensive pic-

ture of ferocious hate ; but confine myself to
the detail of its results.

It was agreed that we should commence
the combat with our pistols, and, if they failed,
we were to determine it by our swords. The
ground was measured, and, at the distance of
eight paces, my antagonist and I stood face
to face. Our seconds had arranged that the
challenged party should fire first. We were
asked if we were prepared, and having replied in the affirmative, the signal was given.
I saw the flash, and trembled to and fro for
a few seconds, then fell backward on the
earth : the ball of my foe had passed through
my body.

Dreadful, excruciating were the sensations
which I endured during the few succeeding

minutes, while I lay on the grass—the *crimson* grass, which I had prophesied should be the bed of my enemy. In spite of the great effusion of blood, which, conjoined to what I had previously lost, induced a mortal weakness, I yet retained a vivid consciousness of all that passed around me.

My antagonist had thrown the discharged pistol on the earth, and stood with his arms folded across his breast, regarding with a stern and fixed countenance the wound from which my life-blood was fast issuing. Motionless and impenetrable as a statue, it was impossible to infer from his impassive countenance the nature of his feelings; but he appeared to be awaiting the result without anxiety, and without exultation.

My second advanced to assist me; but I

snatched the handkerchief from his grasp,
and applied it myself to the wound. An increased feebleness then subdued me, and I fell
back on the grass, still keeping my eyes fixed
on the countenance of my adversary, who retorted with an equally immoveable gaze.

I had thus lain during what appeared to
me an eternity, but in reality, perhaps, did
not exceed a couple of minutes, when his
second approached him, and advised him to
depart.

"No, no!" I shrieked in the agony of my
dread lest my anticipated victim should escape
me: " stay, stay, I command you!—I am
prepared, and capable of firing;" and I presented my pistol.

But the second of my adversary interfered,
and stated that so long as I remained prostrate

on the ground, the laws of duelling required that I should be considered *hors de combat;* and that unless I arose, he could not consent that my foe should sustain my fire.

My friend then approached, in the intention of aiding me to rise; but the opposing second again intervened, and declared that unless I could stand, and fire without assistance, he should remove his principal from the ground.

I groaned with anguish; and nothing, I fear, prevented me from sending my bullet through the head of this zealous adviser, but the dread of thereby suffering my far more hated antagonist to escape. I instigated my second to protest against the injustice of this proceeding; but his remonstrances were vain; for, as we both too well knew the other was

acting in accordance with the common rules
and precedents on these occasions.

During this discussion, I was momentarily
growing weaker. Hastily, therefore, in the
fear of becoming utterly incapacitated, I struggled to rise, and partially succeeded, but immediately fell again. A second time, I made
a still more violent effort, and contrived, with
the assistance of the pistol, to raise myself on
one knee. But the pain I then suffered was
excruciating, and the great difficulty was yet
to be surmounted. How vividly intense, even
at this moment, is my recollection of the
scene. My foe was still intently regarding
me with the same impassive, inscrutable gaze.
Not an emotion was apparent in the stony
rigidity of his fixed and pale features. He
neither quailed beneath my wrathful glances,

nor retorted with a similar expression. His dark, deep-set eyes seemed to penetrate the inmost recesses of my soul, but offered no clue to the secrets of his own.

At length I succeeded in attaining my feet. For a moment I reeled as though in a state of utter ebriety; then with one final, I may almost say, superhuman exertion of my remaining strength, I stood for a single moment as firm and motionless as a rock, deliberately levelled my pistol at his throat, and fired. With the fierce shriek of the death-agony he sprang convulsively into the air, and with a dull heavy sound fell on the earth a corpse. I saw the result—saw that my prophecy was fulfilled, that the green grass was *red* beneath him, uttered a faint cry of exultation, and sank into the arms of my second.

But another spectacle was yet reserved for me. I was aroused by a shriek so fierce, so terrible, that it might have awakened the dead on the judgment-day. Before me, prostrate on the ground, with the body of her brother intertwined in her embrace, her white garments and hair dabbled in blood, lay the unfortunate object of my love and my wrath. Suddenly she sprang to her feet with the rapidity of lightning, and raised her bare and crimsoned arm in threatening denunciation against me. I heard not her words; every faculty was benumbed; and motionless, speechless, fascinated as though under the influence of a basilisk, I gazed in awe unutterable on this sight of horror. With the red spot of frenzy on her forehead, her pallid cheek, contracted brow, dilated nostril, and

quivering lip, she looked the personification
of War, or the type of the Destroying Angel.
The hair bristled on my head; my eyes became infected by the weakness of my brain;
her form seemed to dilate until it stood above
me like a tower, and I swooned beneath my
terror and my agony.

For many after weeks I lay suspended between life and death.   Often the natural
strength of my constitution made an effort
which would have restored me, but the moment I returned to my senses, the violence
and impetuosity of my feelings induced an
agitation which invariably renewed my dis-
order with redoubled force.   She, whom in
the perversion of my heart I then believed to
be the unhappy source of all my woes and
all my crimes, was the incessant object of

my thoughts and my inquiries. But I could gain no information with regard to her. Since the fatal day of her brother's death, she had never been seen to quit the house of her father; and none of the neighbourhood knew aught of the privacy of her life, save that she existed in solitude and in sorrow.

The family of my opponent having declined to take any legal steps to avenge his death, when I recovered, I was spared the necessity of concealment, or the pain and shame of a public trial. The first use I made of my restored strength and freedom was in personally endeavouring to acquire some account of her. By conciliation, by bribery, by stratagem, I strove to obtain from the servants whom I could encounter, the knowledge of any domestic incident, however trivial, which related to her. But all my attempts were vain. I could learn, indeed, that she was clad in black; that she was frequently discovered in convulsive grief, and that she rarely left her chamber; but nothing of her conduct which could enable me to form the remotest surmise with regard to the sentiments she might now entertain for me. Neither in the agony of her sorrow, nor in the violence of her indignation, could any one declare that she had been heard to mention the name, or even to allude to the existence of her brother's murderer.

Hour after hour, and day after day, have I passed in wandering round her father's domain, in the vague hope of discerning her light form in the distance, or even of tracing a vestige of her step in the long grass, or on the gravelly soil. Evening has again arrived; yet still have I staid loitering with the same indefinite and deceptive feeling, gazing on the window of her chamber, until the light that rendered it visible was extinguished: then, I retired to curse the folly of my pursuit, and to rue that I was born. In storm and in calm, in heat and in cold, this was the occupation of my nights and days.

How wild and vain were then my fancies! How often, while I wandered through the thick darkness with my strained eyes eternally fixed on that inaccessible light, have I thought on the tales of the eastern poets, and on the legends of our own land, and longed to have existed in the times when I might have bartered my soul with Eblis, or Beelzebub, for a flying Car, or winged Girdle, that would have enabled me to hover for but one moment around that illuminated window. My mind has even become so utterly enervated by despondency, that more than once I seriously recalled to my recollection the superstition of my school-days, when I believed that the recital of Christ's prayer, *backwards,* was a spell that would summon the Evil One from his den; and I felt almost inclined to practise the absurd impiety.

But what was the source of this exquisite interest? Was it love of her? or, was it love of revenge? Did I wish to woo her? or, did I wish to devote her to the fate of her brother? I was inflamed by neither of these motives separately, but by a combination of them all, and of all the inconsistent passions which ever agitated the human breast. I revered her many virtues, but I loathed her fickleness; for, in the perversity of my blindness, even to this base quality, which dwells but in feeble or in vitiated minds, did I attribute her abandonment of me. I desired, to retain her love, but I still more desired to make her atone for the sorrow and the guilt which she had entailed upon me. I adored her as the source of former bliss, but I detested her as the origin of my present misery.

These were the opposing sensations which she excited in me; and under their torturing influence I knew not where to turn to hide me from myself. I writhed too under the shame of conscious weakness; for I felt that

Fate had indeed separated us for ever. The sister could never be the wife of the brother's murderer.

After a prolonged endurance of these maddening conflicts, I at length gained sufficient strength to enable me to resolve to quit the country, and remain in foreign lands until I should recover a more healthful tone of mind. Having a relative in Smyrna engaged in extensive trade, 1 determined to join him, embark in his speculations, and endeavour to obliterate, in the suspense and excitation of commercial pursuits, all recollection of my previous life.

But, before I departed, I sought to leave my sting behind me. I wrote the following letter, which I contrived should be delivered to her after I had sailed.

" Your curse is upon me; and like Cain, a fugitive and a vagabond, I am about to wander over the surface of the earth. The voice of thy brother's blood crieth up to me from the ground; and I, too, can reply, in the beautifully pathetic language of Scripture, ' My punishment is greater than I can bear.'

" When first I knew you, whatever I might previously have been, I was walking in the path of rectitude; I sinned neither in deed nor in thought. If not inspired by any enthusiastic passion for virtue, yet my mind was in a state of quiescence, which habit and reflection might have strengthened into a religious stability.

" You appeared, and my whole nature changed; my slumbering energies were awakened, and I laid them at your feet, for you to direct to good or evil. How you have fulfilled this trust, ask your own heart.

" Others have a thousand pursuits : ambition, pleasure, all the paths of wisdom, or frivolity, are open before them. In policy, in literature, in art, in all the various professions, men have a stake and an interest, and toil for gold, power, or renown. But I possessed none of these resources, virtuous or vicious. I had set my life upon a cast; I had but one thought, one object in existence; and, directly or indirectly, every action, every desire was associated with it. *You* were that object; and in you were comprised *my* life, and *my* world. Again, I demand you to ask yourself, how you have replied to this devotion?

" Now, hear my answer. On the showing

of an aggrieved, and therefore a partial, witness, you learn the crime of my youth. Your
blood is inflamed by this exaggerated statement; and, without considering that the man
may regret the errors of the boy, you indulge
the impetuosity of your vindictiveness. This
was not just; yet, so far, your conduct was
comparatively venial. But my tale ends not
here. Remorselessly, relentlessly, in spite of
the most abject humiliation, though I stood
before you in heart-broken penitence, and solemnly warned you of the consequences of
your implacability—warned you, that on
your decision depended the lives of two and
the salvation of one—yet, in cold-blooded
self-possession, when the delirium of passion
was past, deliberately, callously you cast me
off from you for ever. This was your deed;

and verily it has met—ay, and shall continue to meet—its reward.

" What may be my future fate, I know not : but should sorrow and suffering so far undermine the little moral strength which remains to me, as to induce me to perpetrate the last, and weakest act of human folly, believe, and tremble at my prophecy,—Hereafter, my blood will be required at your hands.

" Ponder on what I have written—and live —live for ever—to lament that you were born." ——

In framing this letter, I was the victim of contending emotions. The love which I still felt for her, perpetually instigated me to introduce expressions of tenderness and charity; but, my misanthropy prevailed. I looked on myself, and I said, Behold what she has made me! And is *she*, the cause of all, to be exempt from retribution? Am *I* to be the only victim? No! let her drink, and drink to the dregs, of the waters she has herself spontaneously imbittered!

And I smiled exultingly as I pictured to myself her cheek of health—her radiant eye—her elastic step—her soft and blooming cheek, converted into sickliness and emaciation—into sorrow and prostration: and I anticipated the bliss of saying, This is my work.

During my voyage, I vainly endeavoured to withdraw my thoughts from the consideration of this all-painful theme. I struggled, and struggled intrepidly and consistently; but the curse of rejection was on me; and I writhed beneath its fatal infliction. Love, hatred, pride, shame, pity, and vengeance, were the conflicting passions which made my breast the arena for their strife, and retained both body and mind in an equal state of unmanly enervation.

We arrived at Smyrna; and I immediately plunged into all the intricacies of commercial speculation. My attention was most assiduous; and I devoted the whole of the day to the execution of the schemes which I often passed the night in projecting. This application was the result of my strong determination to struggle against my thoughts; but, I believe, had my mind been unoccupied, that I should naturally have derived a gratification from this pursuit; for in its excitation, its comprehensiveness, there was something peculiarly congenial to the general tone of my character.

The unreserved confidence of my uncle was speedily gained; and before I had passed six months in laboriously and consistently perfecting myself in the routine and detail of business, he entrusted me with the entire control of his extensive negotiations.

Then I felt a sort of diplomatic spirit arise within me; a love of intrigue, calculation, and of the arrangement of all that mental machinery which directs and governs gigantic schemes in their remotest ramifications. Instigated by an ambition naturally as boundless as that of a Goertz, a Ripperda, or an Al-

beroni, had Fate in earlier life afforded me an
opportunity for its development, I endeavoured
to make the success of the last speculation but
a means of increasing the magnitude of the
succeeding one. In every instance, without
exception, Fortune favoured my exertions.
War raged throughout Europe, but never
was a ship of ours captured; they usually
sailed to and fro the crowded seas without
meeting an enemy; but, if they did, they
escaped; or, as occurred more than once,
the merchant ship repulsed the armed vessel.
Hurricanes, fire, all the casualties attached
to our profession, passed heedlessly, harmlessly over us; scarcely could we believe
that such dangers existed. Perhaps neither
Jacques Cœur, nor Cosmo de' Medici ever

conducted a more prosperous or extensive commerce.

Thus was I occupied during nearly two years; but then the stimulus failed. By the continued exertion of my energy, I had hitherto repressed that foe of my peace, the one great passion of my heart; but, alas, I too soon discovered that I had suspended, not weakened its power. Occasionally I unwittingly lost myself in recurrences to the past; in dreams of love, regret, and of anticipated vengeance; but I would rouse myself from the thrall, and rush into the tumult and abstraction of my worldly pursuits. Yet night —night, the fell tyrant, with its solitude, and its calm, its blackness, and its sleeplessness, I could not escape. When once the thought of home, and of *her*, had seized on my prostrated mind, I wandered again through the green woods, on the hill, in the valley, and then—I lay in hopeless torture, the unresisting victim of my remorse, my love, and my hate, until the blessed light of dawn, and the voices and stir of men, arose to my succour, with their gaiety and their life.

And yet, as though my grief was not suf-ficent, I possessed an artificial mode of foster-ing it. During the commencement of our intimacy, one lovely autumnal day, while walking in her garden, I discerned her from the summit of an adjoining eminence, and in fear and trembling advanced to meet her. She received me courteously, though formally, and we were pursuing a desultory, and some-what restrained discourse, when she plucked

a flower from that beautiful plant the scabious.
Professing to be ignorant of its perfume, I
made a motion as though I would willingly
have withdrawn it from her grasp, if I had
dared. Confused and surprised, uncertain
whether she ought to dissent or comply, in
the indecision of her action, our hands met; I
seized the flower, and in spite of all my re-
verence and all my timidity, never returned
it. That evening I reached my home, thrilling
in every nerve and vein with pleasure and
exultation.

This flower I had artificially dried, and had
ever since guarded with such care that after
the lapse of three years, it was still in a state
of perfect preservation. It accompanied me
on my voyage; and during my sojourn in the
East, many and many a bitter hour have I

endured in contemplating it. Divided by so
vast a distance, and still more widely by force
of circumstance, it were vain to attempt to
depict the sad, the painful, the dreadful
thoughts engendered by this little memorial
of hope, of home, and of happiness. None
but an ardent lover can estimate the extent of
its power in imparting a vividness to the past.
It was a relic that addressed itself to the most
powerful senses; one that I could see, that I
could scent, that I could touch. It seemed
to carry me through time and space into
actual contact with her who had gathered it;
and again, and again, without any effort of
volition, was acted before me the scene I have
described. In the delicious climate of the
East, amid every inducement to repose and
enjoyment, and surrounded by all the en-

chantment and luxury which that enchanted
and luxurious land can alone supply; beneath
the glittering dome of the gorgeous palace;
in the fairy garden, by the side of the fountain,
with its marble columns of exquisite whiteness in beautiful union with the noble foliage
of the date, the palm, and the pomegranate
tree; while the Persian sang, and the dark-
eyed, graceful Georgian danced beneath the
liquid light of the silver moon, have 1 sat
gazing on that little flower until my sorrow
rose in my throat, and I felt as though my
heart-strings would have cracked. And yet
such was my infatuation, that though this
memorial of past happiness but served to aug-
ment my anguish, I never could acquire the
fortitude to abandon, or destroy it.

To this extent, however, had I succeeded

in controlling the dictates of my passion, neither directly, nor indirectly, in any of my letters, had I ventured to allude to her. Though no previous communication on the subject had occurred between us, my sisters, my principal correspondents, seemed to feel the force of this omission ; for they never informed me of aught that in the remotest degree related to her, or to her family : and despite the temptations which I repeatedly endured, this silence remained inviolate.

I had passed two entire years in the East when my uncle died, bequeathing to me the whole of his immense wealth and extensive trade. Then came upon me an indomitable desire of returning to England. Yielding to the impulse which I could not control, and mentally attempting to palliate my weakness

by the adoption of the Oriental creed, that
man is born to fulfil his destiny, I prepared
to return to the land of my birth. During
the few ensuing months, I was as industriously
engaged in contracting the dealings of our
house, as I had previously been in enlarging
them. At length, having converted the
greater portion of my merchandize into gold,
and so limited and arranged my commercial
transactions as to enable a confidential agent
to conduct them with safety, I departed from
the East.

The hand of disease was still upon me; I
had never recovered the blow which I had
received. The pernicious effects of an ener-
vating climate, the anxieties which I endured,
and the exertions which I made in the se-
dulous prosecution of my arduous avocation,

all tended to prolong the malady engendered by a wounded frame and a broken heart: and I stepped on my native shore, dejected and careworn, hopeless, fearless, reckless—a man without a smile, and without a tear.

Great were the changes which I found that my family had experienced. My only surviving parent had been dead several months; and I afterwards learned that the letter which bore me this afflicting intelligence had arrived in Smyrna on the very day I quitted it. My elder sister, married to a man of rank and affluence, had gone to reside in the metropolis; and my younger sister, warned by me of my approaching return, alone remained to welcome me to the home of my fathers.

But great as were these changes, how much greater were those which the family of my

H

unfortunate mistress had experienced. For
many months after the death of his son,
her father had led a life as secluded as
that of his daughter. At last, instigated
perhaps by the hope of excitement and dis-
traction, he embarked a small portion of his
fortune in mercantile adventure. He was
eminently successful; and impelled by his
success, he was induced to enter into some
mining speculations of enormous magnitude.
The consequence was, that, on my return to
England, I found him utterly ruined. His
estate, his last remaining property, was announced for public sale; and in the course of
two short weeks, he and his daughter, would
be driven from it, friendless, houseless men-
dicants, to live, or starve, on the narrow gifts
of contumelious charity.

And how did I receive this information?—
With utter, unalloyed exultation! But let
it not be thought that I hoped to revenge
my supposed wrongs by persecution; no, for
I hoped to revenge them still more deeply
by kindness. I sought to fortify, not to
weaken her affection; I sought to punish
her through the self-reproaches of her own
heart, not through any external infliction: I
sought to force her to believe that she had
been the spontaneous source of our mutual
unhappiness; and I only rejoiced in her ruin,
because I anticipated that it would afford me
an opportunity of overwhelming her with
benefits, and of exciting in her a sense of
painful and hopeless gratitude. Miserable as
I was, my misery would have been increased
even a hundred-fold, had I been assured that

she had ceased to love me; for, in defiance of
my crime and of my violence, I deduced from
the intensity of her former affection, the enthusiasm and tenderness of her nature, and
the solitude of her life—which, offering no
theme for present contemplation, forces the
mind to dwell on the memory of the past—
that, despite of all her efforts to eradicate it,
she must still retain her passion for me. Thus,
with a ruthless exultation, I had long been
accustomed to dwell on the idea, that at some
future, perhaps, not distant period of my life,
I should experience that greatest earthly happiness of seeing her at my feet, and of then
contemning her proffered love as she had rejected mine. Little, however, did I purpose
to persist in this contempt; I meant but to
mete unto her as she had meted unto me, and

then to take her to my bosom, and devote the
rest of my days to eradicate the impression of
the past—to force her to say that the last
state of this man is *not* worse than the first.
These were my dreams, and fearful was their
realization.

In prosecution of these intentions, I pur-
chased through a confidential agent, the entire estate of her father. At a very large
pecuniary sacrifice, I paid all his debts, and
placed him again in uncontrolled possession
of his property ; working so secretly, that no
effort of his could ever have enabled him to
trace the hand to which he was indebted. But
I was aware that they knew of my return ;
and I left her to *feel* that I was their bene-
factor. None but those who have possessed
passions such as mine, can imagine the wild

and proud pleasure I derived from this first exercise of my power over her who had seen me at her feet and trampled on my contrition.

For several months after these occurrences, I patiently awaited some manifestation, direct or indirect, from her or her parent, of their consciousness that I was the author of them. I haunted as before, in gloom and despondency, the environs of the park; but I could not even obtain a glimpse of her form. After the fatal duel, all intercourse between our families had ceased; no hostility had been exhibited, but my sisters naturally felt that the sight of them could not but be painful to the bereaved father and daughter.

But, heedless of this honorable delicacy, and instigated by the agony of my impatience, I now prevailed upon my sister to visit their solitary abode. She was received with solemn courtesy; and at the end of a long half hour she returned to fill me with despair.

Often, with a reckless profaneness, had I said unto myself, Behold and see! there is no sorrow like unto my sorrow! but the tale of my sister proved the fallacy of my judgment: I had not yet known what Heaven destined me to bear. She described a painful change in the appearance of both father and daughter; she dwelt on the fixed gloom which had engraven itself on her features; on the tones of their voices, the sombre character of their demeanour, their heart-breaking dejection and prostration of spirit. She had availed herself of an opportunity of mentioning my name: the father started beneath the sound, but the daughter exhibited no emotion.

"With the beautiful resignation and sub-
lime suffering of a saint," pursued my sister,
" she seems only to exist in the anticipation
of a future state, and to regard herself as
eternally severed from the ties which bind
frail mortality to the earth. She recalls
to me the picture I saw, when in Paris with
my sister, of that lovely but erring lady, La
Valière, in her conventual garments, suppli-
cating her Creator to sustain her in her hour
of affliction. Though dissimilar in feature,
precisely the same heavenly expression of
humility, benevolence, and exquisite sorrow,
beams in the large, humid, and yet pellucid
eye of both. Believe me, my dear brother,
that for worlds I would not willingly distress
you; but you really must suffer me to say,
that I cannot conceive a sight more touch-

ingly pathetic, more painfully interesting, than this afflicted father and daughter."

The words of my sister smote me to my heart, and for a time I remained plunged in bitter retrospection : but, soon recovering myself, I multiplied question on question, to endeavour to extract some evidence of the nature of the feelings with which I might now inspire her. But I could derive no consolation from the answers ; not a word, look, or tone, had revealed the shadow of even a passing interest in my existence.

" Why torment yourself by these inquiries, my brother ?" cried my sister : " I will not affect to be ignorant of their motive, and the love I bear you would induce me to deceive you, but that I believe it is better for your happiness that you should know the truth.

Unreservedly, then, will I confess to you that
I watched her narrowly for your sake; and
you know the piercing power of a woman's
eye, in detecting the secrets of the heart in her
own sex, is proverbial—*nous nous ressem-
blons toutes, et nous connoissons notre secret.* I fear, then, I do not err, when I say,
that I am convinced that *the past can never
be recalled.* I think she has endeavoured to
banish you from her mind; but, if you ever recur to it, I *am sure* that the image induces no
pleasurable feelings. I speak thus sincerely
and thus harshly to you, my dear brother, because I loathe to see you pining and fretting in
the indulgence of a fallacious hope, wasting a
life that might be useful to others, and happy
and honorable to yourself. Believe me,
teach yourself that you are separated for

ever, and your natural strength of mind will emancipate you from the fetters of this unmanly despondency."

My sister judged truly. Hitherto I had only existed in the idea that she *must* still retain her affection for me in her inmost soul, however much the exhibition of it might be suppressed. But now, and now only, I began to suggest to myself the possibility, nay, the more than probability, of her having ceased to love me. Like the Sirocco, the thought swept across my heart, and left all desolate.

Nerved by desperation no longer to endure the agony of suspense, that same morning I addressed a letter to her, which I commanded, with the most threatening injunctions, my messenger to fail not himself to place in her hands. My order was obeyed; and, during the evening, my letter was returned to me *unopened.*

From that hour I became the prey of the combined tortures of hopeless love and hopeless hatred. I wandered about, a miserable man; and I stood with my head bowed on my breast, and I cried, " From Dan even to Beersheba, all, all is barren." My spirit raged against my kind; and I wished that all animate nature could be concentrated beneath my foot, that I might enjoy the ecstasy of crushing it into annihilation. And yet, such is the inconsistency of all human passions, that I, who could entertain these savage thoughts, who could ruthlessly raise my hand against the life of another, and as fearlessly stake my own on the flight of a bullet or the thrust of a sword, have yet stood trembling over the lake, the pistol, or the poison, contemplating the suicide which I sought, but dared not to commit!

How often, then, in my moments of calmer anguish, has the selfish and painful thought of the hours and days, the months and years which I had so fruitlessly consumed; of the love, devotion, and energy which I had so fruitlessly lavished, made me recall to myself, and feel in its fullest force and beauty, the exquisite pathos of that most touching speech which history records, "If I had served my God as I have served my king, he would not have forsaken me in these my gray hairs!"

But in the absorption of this painful recurrence to one of the severest trials of even my unhappy life, I must not omit to pay a tribute of affection to the memory of my fond

sisre.t Oh, woman, woman! much calum-
niated being by the frivolous and the prosperous, in the hour of adversity we feel and
admit the consciousness of your superiority.
The lover assiduously attends the sick bed of
his mistress; the son bewails and caresses his
dying parent; and friend cleaves to friend
with persevering regard: the surface is fair,
but beneath is the lurking, secret, sometimes,
perhaps, even half unconscious, hope of present or future personal benefit. Woman,
woman alone, is capable of genuine unalloyed
disinterestedness; and for her alone is reserved the high honor of proving that self-love
is *not* the sole motor of existence.

Of this nature was my devoted sister: she
adored virtue for virtue's sake; and really
believed that the practice of it induced its

own reward. She saw that I was miserable, far, far beyond the common apportionment of misery; and though, as I afterwards knew, she was at that very time sincerely attached to a neighbouring gentleman of high mind, birth, and character, who felt for her a more than equal affection, yet she cheerfully withdrew herself from the indulgence of this natural and fascinating feeling, to devote herself to my consolation; not as man may sometimes sacrifice to man in the rigid performance of a self-imposed duty, but in the beautiful unconsciousness of heavenly impulse.

While this beloved girl thus attempted, though in vain, to sooth the wretchedness of my state, the father of her who had indirectly caused it died; brought down to a premature

grave by the misfortunes he had endured.
In spite of her apparent hostility, all that
related to her was still a subject of painful
interest to me; and deeply did I lament the
grief which I knew this fresh wound would
occasion her.

A few weeks after this event, I had been
sitting during several successive hours on the
spot where we had first met; above me, was
the intertwined foliage, and below me, was the
rapid stream.   Oh! bitterly, bitterly painful
was the chain of thought which this location
suggested! And yet, with the infatuation of
a morbid mind, pursuing the current of my
miserable reflections, I continued to contrast
the past with the present moment. Again
and again I arrayed before myself all the
minutest circumstances which related to that

scene. I pictured her sunny smile, her beaming eye, her classic form in congenial union
with her classic harp; and I dwelt on her
sacred melody, until " *Madre amata*," and
each plaintive note, appeared again to tremble
on my ear. These were the reminiscences
which I tortured myself by placing in com-
parison with my actual state.

Wrapt in the corroding anguish of this
retrospection, I grew scarcely conscious of
time or place, when suddenly a sound of
singular interest aroused me into attention;
it seemed the half-suppressed sob of female
grief. I listened intently; it *was* a woman's
voice bewailing; and now, borne on the
breeze, came a louder and a deeper burst of
sorrow. Excited instantaneously by a feeling
which I could not define, into a temporary

I

self-oblivion, I stole cautiously along until I obtained a sight of the sufferer.

God of heaven! for the first time for four long years I stood within a few yards of the being I adored! I knew—I felt that it was she, though I saw not her face. Clinging to the next branch for support, I gazed with a full and bursting soul on the picture she presented—and oh! how piteous, and yet how beautiful it was!

She was seated beneath the trunk of an old and fantastic tree, the huge limbs of which inclining downwards, its thick foliage threw a soft shadow around her. A simple garment of white, not ample enough to conceal the graceful outline of her Phidian form, displayed a neck of dazzling and exquisitely voluptuous whiteness. One statue-like arm,

bare to the shoulder, uniting all the fulness
and polish of the purest marble with the softness of nature, hung by her side, while the
hand, as perfect in symmetry as in hue,
rested lightly on the turf. The other pressed
her forehead, which, bowed to her knees, was
concealed by the dishevelled hair that fell in
heavy masses to the earth, where it lay in
accumulated clusters of silken brilliancy. She
sighed and moaned most piteously; and heart-
rending were the sobs which momentarily
convulsed her frame, as she rocked to and
fro, with an irregular and painful motion, in
the strong agony of her grief.

This was the spectacle that met my gaze;
and had it been the fabled Medusa, I could
not have been more quickly transformed into
stone. My blood ceased to flow, my pulse

to beat; and I stood a breathless statue, in all but the too vivid consciousness of pity, horror, and remorse.

Suddenly, with fearful vehemence, she cast herself on her knees, and clasping her hands, raised her lovely arms to heaven in energetic prayer. I heard not her words; but the action and the expression denoted the homage of a broken and of a bleeding heart. She ceased; and her arms fell by her side, her head sank on her breast; the parted lips were motionless, and she seemed for a few moments in all the supineness of overwhelming despair: then, abruptly starting to her feet, she took one long lingering survey of earth and sky, and dashed herself into the stream. The agitated waters seized on her fragile form, and enveloped her in their gloomy depths;

then tossing her to their surface, bore her rapidly along their raging course of foam and whirlpool.

What followed I know not, until I found myself standing on the brink of the stream, with her senseless body in my arms. In the madness of that moment, all reason was lost, and I had acted from intuitive and unconscious impulse.

I laid her on the grass, and essayed every remedy that art or affection could suggest to restore her to life, but in vain; till, frantic with disappointment, in a paroxysm of grief, I threw myself by her side, and insanely kissed her lips, her eyes, and her forehead. The blood began to dance in my veins like burning alcohol, and the pent-up passions of years burst their unnatural confinement. I

wound my arms around her unresisting form;
I clasped her to my heart with the strong
pressure of delirium, and yet I felt as though
I only grasped a vision, a vacancy; substance
itself was not enough substantial, reality not
enough real, to glut the insatiate cravings of
this fierce transport of blended love and grief.
None, but those who may have possessed
passions as ungovernable as mine, can picture
the savage, the fearful delight which I derived from this clandestine embrace of what
I then conceived to be the living and the
dead!

There she lay before me; she, whom during
four long years I had vainly endeavoured
even to behold. There she lay; she, the
pure, the rigid, the inflexible, without a tone
or a gesture to check the wildest expression

of my love. And yet, there was the form, and there was the eye, which had once inspired me with the very intensity of that causeless fear which arises in the excess of passionate affection. "And now," I cried, raising her arm, and then allowing it to drop heavily on the earth, " the ruled has become the ruler, the slave is converted into the despot. I, the trembler, have now but to command, and lo, I am obeyed. I have but to say, Do this, and it doeth it;" and again I raised the arm, and waved it in the air, in awful mockery of the action of life.

But a flood of tears, and bitter agonizing dejection, soon succeeded to this ebullition of all the ferocious and inhuman passions of my nature. I pressed her hand to my face, I

bowed my head to the earth, and I wept like
a child.

While wrapt in the bitterness of my grief,
I thought that I felt a convulsive movement
in the hand enclosed in mine. I gazed intently on her face, and distinctly discerned a
quivering in the lips. In a transport of hope,
I raised her in my arms, and bore her to my
home. Medical assistance was immediately
summoned; and before two hours had elapsed
she was restored to life. Swayed by the advice of my sister, and by my own dread of
the effect which the sight of me might produce
on her in her still precarious state, I retired
to my room, before she was sufficiently recovered to recognize the objects around her.

In anxiety and agitation, I was revolving

this extraordinary event, speculating on its cause, and endeavouring to surmise its results, when a servant entered, and presented me with a letter which had just been brought by a messenger from the hall. I started in astonishment, and a thrill of painful expectation ran through my veins, as I gazed on her well-known hand. I observed that it bore the date of the previous day ; and then, in doubt and fear, in hope and eagerness, with a trembling hand, and an unsteady eye, proceeded to read that which follows.

" When this last confession of a fated sinner shall be revealed to you, the spirit of her who penned it shall be hovering around you, shall be searching into your heart, shall be striving to commune with you : and if ever

Heaven allowed the laws of mortal nature to
be broken for any other than its own great
purposes, doubt not that its presence shall be
manifest to you. You shall feel it breathe on
your soul, and blend with your being.

" Bashful, irresolute, apprehensive, the hereditary slave of prejudice and education, woman's career, from generation to generation,
is one of continued self-deceit, mistrust, and
restraint. But now, standing on the verge of
the grave, the betrothed of death, with eyes
that pierce into space, and meet on every tree
the beckoning antics of the impatient fiend,
the iron trammels of factitious habit fall from
my mind, and I glory in declaring that—*I
adore you*. I discard the timidity of my nature and the pride of my sex, and I avow exultingly, that I linger with delight, as I slowly

retrace the three little, but oh, how compre-
hensive words, *I adore you!*

" And yet, none can ever know how I have
struggled with my passion, how I have schooled
myself to repress it.   Often in an agony of remorse have I passed the sleepless night and
day in imploring the protection of Heaven;
but it came not.   Eve after eve, morn after
morn, when I offered up my homage to my
Creator, I have sworn to forget you; but I
only slept to dream of you, or awakened to
summon before me, incident by incident, the
blissful detail of our too fleeting intercourse.
Nowhere could I turn for succour.   With
every action of my life, with every operation
of nature, some thought of you was indelibly
associated.   The rising and the setting sun,
the green hills, the gentle gale, the moon, the

stars, the scent of flowers, all were so many
foes to my peace, for all served in turn but to
remind me of you. My books I dared not
open, and music was even more fertile in
heart-breaking recollection.

" *Strife*—constant, ceaseless, internal strife
is the history of my life since we parted. And
yet, so potent was the effect of my early self-
discipline, that during the whole of this eternity of suffering, nor word nor look has ever
betrayed the weakness of my heart. God
only knows what this effort has cost me, nor
what I have endured, when I have marked
you wandering beneath my window, in re-
pressing my desire to offer you some token
of my pardon and affection. Ah, relentless,
vindictive, implacable, must you then have
deemed me; and little did you think, while

thus you dissipated health and happiness in the fruitless hope of gazing upon me, the callous, the obdurate, that I passed the equal hour in furtively watching your course, and sympathising in your anguish—that I gave you sigh for sigh, and groan for every groan.

" Bitter, oh bitter were those moments of trial! How often, then, did I repeat to myself, that but for my own insensate rashness, my guilty violence, this desolation had never been. Our world was a garden of flowers, and I wantonly laid it waste. My poor, poor brother! I may not, *could* not if I would, criminate his noble, honest nature; but I cannot consent to die, and suffer you to think me more culpable than I am. The tale of your early life was repeated to me in a moment of excitation, and I have since too often felt that

he may unconsciously have exaggerated the
errors of your conduct. Well do I now remember that he described you with an animosity of which I did not deem him capable;
but, alas! I knew not then of your encounter
and contest on the morn of that very eve, or
I might have received his statement with the
modification of suspicion. Oh, that it had
pleased Heaven to have enlightened me; I
might not now have to lament a brother's
loss, or to turn to the east and the west, the
north and the south, but find no succour.

" Think not that I would attempt to justify
my conduct; I seek but to make you regard
it in its proper light. No; heinous has been
my crime, and fearful must be the atonement!

" So long as my poor father remained, I,
too, was doomed to support the infliction of

existence. But now that he has left this hap-
less scene, unshackled, unfettered, free as air,
I reign the queen of myself; more despotic
than the despot, for *he* but rules another's life,
while *I* have attained dominion of my own.
I love you—I adore you—and—we are separated for ever! A red stream flows between
us—it haunts me by day, and it follows me
by night. Beyond it I see happiness, elysium,
—but I *may* not pass. On this side is despair; on the other, hope, love, gratitude,
sympathy, all the blessings of this mortal
state; but still I *may* not cross that small
dark line of eternal disunion—for it is *my
brother's blood.* This course alone, then, remains for my adoption—the sister dare not
wed her brother's murderer, but she dares to

die rather than live apart from him whom she
more than idolizes.

" Now I have unlocked the inmost secrets
of my heart; it is as naked before you as
before my Creator. Oh, your curse is indeed
upon me !—' I *do* live to lament that I was
born !'—Harsh as was that wish, still harsher
was the cause you had for framing it.   I felt
that I deserved it at your hands, and I wept
bitter tears over my picture of the agony in
which it must have originated.   The rest of
your letter but increased my sympathy and
affection, for I saw in every line the excess of
your despair, and I pardoned, nay, almost
loved, that acerbity of expression which served
but to prove your deep sense of your loss.
To me you have ever been all that is good :

and oh, how I thank you with my whole soul, with all the affection of a fond daughter, and with all the fervour of a grateful woman, for your last generous, noble act of kindness to my poor father! Cease not to remember, that in these sentiments I quitted the world, and let them be a source of consolation to you.

"And now, my beloved, fare you well! Let me entreat, conjure you to school your-self to think of me without regret. Soothing as is to me the expression of these feelings, I never had revealed them, had I not thought that at some future day, you would be less un-happy in the consciousness of them, than if I had quitted this mortal career, allowing you still to suppose me the vindictive, the unjust, the ingrate; the artful winner of your love,

K

and then the contemner of it!—Pray Heaven that in adopting this course I may have judged correctly!

"Shed not one tear over my grave; forget me not, but think on me with serenity. Let my name be to thee an oasis in the desert of memory! And now, may the Almighty restore you to tranquillity, and ultimately to every blessing which this life can offer. Farewell again, then, beloved of my soul, and remember this last, this parting prayer—live, and be happy for my sake."

The moment I had completed the perusal of this powerful and extraordinary picture of love and devotion, of weakness and heroism,

of rectitude and error, of religion and despair, I comprehended that it had never been
intended to have met my eye while the writer
existed; and instantly the whole machinery of
her conduct arrayed itself before me. Unable
longer to struggle against her passion, and
the consequent disgust of life, she had resolved to die. In this determination she had
written the declaration which I had just read,
directing that it should not be delivered into
my hands until after a stated period, when
she contemplated she should no longer belong
to this world of care. She had then left her
home; and but for my intervention her plans
would have been too accurately accomplished.

These were the thoughts that flashed across
me; and then, with the exultation of a fiend,
I strode up and down the chamber, the

eventful letter in my hand. She was mine,
then,—*mine!* bound to me by the ties of
indivisible affection. A free career was open
to me, and I might glut either my love or
my hate. She adored me—had indelibly
recorded her adoration—and I then grasped
that proof of it which admitted of neither
change nor appeal. Was she not beneath
my roof, unprotected, friendless, utterly, irrevocably within my power? Might I not,
then, avail myself of her weakness to effect
her eternal disgrace, and thus at once gratify
the two dearest passions of my heart? Oh,
no! no! worlds should not have tempted me
to have adopted this course. I loved her too
dearly to doom her to endless shame and
misery; but my vindictive, morbid, unhappy
nature, could not forgive her the anguish,

the desolation, which she had caused me.
At that moment, had her life been threatened,
I could have cheerfully sacrificed mine to
have ensured her safety ; but to have pre-
served both, I could not have suppressed my
feelings of resentment. The theory of the
Orientals of two principles, the Good and
the Evil, perpetually waging war in the breast
of man, can alone represent the inconsistency
of my sentiments.

In recurring, after this long lapse of years,
to the deeds of this thrice guilty portion of
my fated career, I sometimes cannot refrain
from fancying that I never could have perpetrated them, unless at the time I had been
the pre-ordained victim of confirmed insanity.
Quem Deus vult perdere prius dementit, is

a maxim which frequently in my own despite occurs to me. But, as this idea brings with it a shadow of consolation, I never allow myself to entertain it; for I am doomed by Heaven and my own will to endure for the remainder of my life the unmitigated horrors of remorse.

While, jaded in mind and body, the prey of intestine strife, I vainly contended with the evil of my heart, repeated messages from the sick chamber informed me of the state of the invalid. Several hours thus elapsed; the evening advanced, and darkness had fallen upon the earth, ere I was gladdened by the entrance of my sister. She told me that her precious charge had been slightly delirious, and had addressed a few incoherent words to those around her, but that she had just sunk into a calm and apparently intense sleep.

Hitherto, my sister had received no explanation of the appearance of her most unexpected guest; but she now sought a solution of the mystery, and I placed the letter in her hand. Her surprise was boundless. Her ingenuous countenance expressed the emotions which its perusal excited, and her deep blushes revealed the woman's sympathy in the feelings of her friend. Her feminine sensibility appeared to be even more struck by its passionate declarations than by its tone of anguish and despair.

When she had read it, she gazed on me with astonishment and inquiry; and I then communicated to her how I had rescued her

friend from self-destruction, and that the
letter had fallen into my possession because
she had not had the power of countermanding
its delivery. My sister listened with attention
and evidently with satisfaction.

"The hand of Providence, brother," she
said, "appears to be in this event: I begin
to think that you may still be happy. What
a noble, though an erring part, has my poor
friend played. She could not live without
you, but she would rather die than wed the
man who was stained with her brother's blood.
How heroic, and yet how weak! how dis-
interested, and yet how selfish! With my
whole soul, I pity her; what a conflict must
have been hers! But, now, it must exist no
longer. With that written witness of the
violence of her affection in your possession,

she cannot again attempt to sever from you. Oh, brother, madly you ought to adore her! How much she is to be admired. Her very frailties are more noble than the virtues of others!"

Though I admitted the justice, or rather the inadequacy of this praise of my sister, yet it grated on my ears, for it was a tacit reproach to the sentiments I entertained. Shunning, therefore, further colloquy on the subject, I repaired to the sick chamber with a cautious step and a throbbing heart; I felt it beat against my chest as though it would have burst its confinement. My whole frame was agitated as with a convulsion; and my trembling limbs would scarcely support me. With emotions ineffable, noiselessly and tenderly I bent over her, and gazed on her dear coun-

tenance. Imperfect as was the light, it was
sufficient to render every object visible. She
lay before me; her head turned toward the
pillow, displayed but a portion of her lovely
face, pale and marble-like, under the influence of exhaustion. Her bright, dark auburne hair, still unconfined, was scattered
around her; and still exposed was her pure
symmetrical arm, that pre-eminently fascinating, but most rare of female charms. So
motionless, so profound her repose, it might
have been deemed the sleep of death, but that
the beauty of life was on her features.

Softly approaching my face still nearer to
hers, I allowed the warm breath to play on
my cheek, until I grew faint beneath the excess of my emotion. Withdrawing a few paces
to recover my self-possession, unwittingly

I again began to reflect on the change which a few short hours had effected in my fortune. When I last beheld her, I deemed myself the fated victim of her barbarity; and now, I stood over her the arbiter of her fate. I could not repress a smile of triumph.

This conflict of passion pursued me during the night. Sometimes I regarded her with all the tenderness of the purest affection; but then again the evil of my heart arose, and steeled me against the united influence of her faith, her love, and her beauty. I only thought of the sufferings I had endured; and that she—*she*, with all her apparent dove-like softness, had been to me as a moral Nemesis, a graven image of Vengeance with heart of iron and claws of brass, a pestilence that goes about seeking whom it may devour. Then,

again, feelings of affection and contrition re-
vived; and, in the bitter consciousness of abject
weakness, I threw myself upon my knees, and
vehemently implored my God to inspire me
with the strength to forego the vindictiveness
I cherished. But Heaven heeded not the
prayers that arose in the despairing ebullitions
of an ill-regulated mind, not in the meek and
lowly spirit of a holy self-abasement; and I
returned to my moody fitful contemplations.
Like Regulus, in his murderous cask, I felt
myself rolling darkly onward to conscious and
certain destruction, but possessed neither the
power of arresting my course, nor of avoiding
the tortures which it inflicted.

*Plus on aime une maîtresse, et plus on est
près de la haïr.* What a strange and startling creed! and yet, when we examine it, we

find it is founded in judgment and truth, and reveals a wondrous knowledge of the human heart. The moderate affection of equable minds, originating in reflection and esteem, is often an enduring one, or tranquilly terminates in natural decay; but that very impetuosity of character and feeling, which is the source of all passionate love, is also a mine of combustible, which any spark may explode into a conflagration of evil. Pitiable is the man who hates her he once adored; but my far more hopeless fate was that perfection, or rather that monster, in misfortune—to love and to loathe, in the same moment, the same object!

> How vast the torments of the mind
>   That struggles to be strong!
> How vast its efforts! yet we find
>   We still pursue the wrong!

In vain our soul its danger knows,
In vain its fate experience shows,
A strength our weakness can't oppose
    Still urges us along!
Until th' exhausted reason seems
O'erta'en by thick and filmy dreams
That darkly press the madden'd brain,
Till wrought into th' excess of pain,
It wakens into sense again!

I knew, I admitted to myself, that I had been born in sin; that, during many years I was innately bad. But, I remembered also that better seed had been sown, and that better thoughts were springing up within me, even before I first met with her. The intercourse which then ensued still farther diminished the influence of the evil spirit upon me; and I felt that on the morn of the accursed interview she had held the scales of my fate; and that a future life of rectitude, or crime, depended on the decision of that moment. This was the bitter, ceaseless reflection which cherished, in defiance of every effort of my better nature, my morbid desire of vengeance.

The night passed, and the day began to gleam through the interstices in the casements. Several times she exhibited symptoms of awakening, and I retired to a part of the chamber, whence I could watch her return to consciousness without being subject to her observation.

She unclosed her lovely eyes and gazed intently around her, but apparently without alarm. She raised herself slowly, and examined every object with increasing attention and surprise. My sister, who had hitherto been partially concealed, now advanced. The

light was still deceptive, and for a few
moments she regarded her with a wildly
scrutinizing, but doubtful gaze; then, suddenly uttering a faint cry of recognition, fell
back on the pillow.

"Dear girl," cried my sister, clasping her
in her arms and passionately embracing her,
"welcome, thrice welcome, to life, to friends,
to happiness!"

. She closed her eyes, and covered her face
with her hands, as though she were incapable
of supporting the wide field of speculation
which these words suggested.

"God of heaven!" she ejaculated in the
low gasping tone of excessive apprehension;
and, after a pause, added slowly and deliberately, with the manner of one nerved by
desperation to ascertain the real extent of the

anticipated danger, " I know that voice—it belongs to one fair and kind, and wise and good—it recalls days of happiness long past. By these, I adjure you, to answer my question. How I have been brought here, I ask not, I seek not to be informed. I recollect too much of a fearful scene to wish that you should now recur to it; but tell me, oh tell me, I implore you, friend of my girlhood, my choice, and of my heart, who is the owner of this abode?"

" A kind and good relative, who——"

" And that relative is——"

" Your friend."

" And— is *your brother?*"

" My brother," replied my sister, hesitatingly.

" Then, I am lost!" she exclaimed with

L

ineffable pathos; but with neither apparent surprise, nor terror.

With a gentle violence, my sister removed her hands from her face, and fondly and soothingly kissed the pale cheeks down which the bright tears followed each other in quick succession. All the fountains of her heart unlocked by this warm sympathy, she drew my sister still closer to her, buried her head in her bosom, and sobbed convulsively. Returning her embrace with redoubled emotion, my affectionate sister mingled her tears with her unhappy friend's. How beautiful are the manifestations of female friendship in the utter self-abandonment of reciprocated sorrow! Never was a more elevating, a more heavenly sight than that then presented by those two lovely girls. And yet, even in that

moment, her rejection, her disdainful *rejection*
—a pestilence on the infernal word!—recurred
to my wounded pride, and filled my soul with
fury.

How calculating is the mind even in its
fiercest passions. Strong as were mine, I
should not, perhaps, have wanted the power
to repress them, had I not been conscious that
she had delivered herself over to me eternally,
irrevocably, and that I might therefore indulge them with impunity.

"Dear friend," exclaimed my sister, "believe me, he adores you. Forget then, your
griefs, exert your energy, and resolve never
to recur to the past. Maintain this resolution for but a few short months, and your
happiness is your own for ever. Rise every
morn to enjoy the day, and to anticipate the

morrow; but, follow the advice which the
wife of Lot neglected, and *dare not look behind.* Come, smile on me, my love, declare
to me that you will comply with my intreaties,
and obliterate, in a long future of contentment,
all recollection of the sorrows that are gone.
·See my brother, express to him these feelings,
and add," continued my sister, smiling through
the vestiges of her tears, " that you love him
almost as much as he loves you."

" Yes," she replied, in a tone half sorrowful,
half resigned, " the time for self-restraint is
past : I can no longer deceive either him or
myself, even if I would. I will see him, and
avow to him the love I bear him."

I advanced and stood before her.

All the blood in her slight form rushed to
her pale face, making every feature incarna-

dined one red; but quickly revelled, and left the countenance of the hue of death.

My sister gazed affectionately on us both, and then left the room. Would to heaven that she had remained! for though love and terror were not strong enough to fetter the demon within me, a feeling of shame might have been more powerful.

With a violent exertion, resisting the impulse which prompted me to throw myself into her arms, I stood moodily gazing on her. In spite of her own emotion, she had sufficient self-possession to discover that I was under the influence of an agitation which the circumstances of our meeting might not have been supposed to engender. A pause ensued; at last, she exclaimed, half affirmatively, half interrogatively,

" You have received a letter?"

" I have."

" You have read it?"

" Yes—a thousand times."

Again she blushed, though not so deeply as before.

" Then I am unmasked!"

" You are indeed; I know every secret nook of your inmost mind and heart."

Surprised more by the tone than by the sentiment of this reply, she looked intently on my face; but she could read there no avowal of the nature of my feelings.

" Why do you gaze so strangely on me, my beloved?" she affectionately exclaimed. " You know—I have confessed—why should I not speak it—my eternal attachment. My fate is decided—abandoned for ever are all

futile attempts at disguise, and—I live only
for you. What then do you apprehend?"
and she added, with female sensitiveness,
" What means this chilling silence?" Then,
with renewed tenderness, she continued, " A
third tie of union exists between us; I long
have owed you love, and gratitude, and now
I owe you a life. My preserver!" she cried,
with enthusiasm, " my preserver from worse
than death, from *crime*, speak to me, I implore you!"

But silently I stood before her; fixedly
regarding her with an impassive, inscrutable
countenance. At last, I replied,

" You owe me no thanks, for my service is
no gift; it is but the payment of a debt. I
once took a life from your house, and now I
return it." Before she could rejoin, I pro-

ceeded with sardonic calmness, " In your im-
passioned letter, I observe, that you never
suppose the very possibility of change in me.
You infer, I conclude, from the many proofs
of affection I persevered in giving so long as
I remained in England, that my passion must
still continue to exist. But do you forget
that two years have since elapsed; and that
I passed them in a land where fidelity is little
honored, and less practised? The women of
the East are ardent as their own sun, beautiful,
and compliant — not callous, haughty, vindictive, and inflexible—not accustomed to
reject the homage of their admirers."

Astonishment, fear, and horror, were blended
on her lovely countenance ; at last, under the
influence of her agony, she exclaimed, addressing herself, rather than me,

" God of heaven! can he—can *he*—have ceased to love me? Have I unsexed myself, discarded all the pride and modesty of woman's nature, to lay the most sacred feelings of the heart at the feet of one who has ceased to value them?—Oh, no! this may not, must not, shall not be!—Answer me, in pity answer me, and tell me, that my suspicions are unfounded!" and as she grasped my hand, the warm tears gushed from her eyes, and fell upon it.

Perhaps, I judge through the medium of my own character, and in the knowledge of my own infirmity; but, I believe, that all our race are more or less ferocious. Many may live and die ignorant that this vice is latent in their breasts; but, because circumstances have not arisen to develop it, let them not therefore believe that they do not possess it. The minds of most of us are capable of a mood in which we should derive a demoniac pleasure from the sight of the tears which we ourselves have caused to trickle down the cheek of beauty. They tell an unquestionable tale of feminine softness, affection, and submission; and man, the savage, revels in the callous complacency of gratified vanity, and in the conviction of his power. There they stand in her bright eyes, visible, tangible, indisputable proofs of her weakness and of his strength, of her homage and of his supremacy; and he gazes on her exultingly, unpityingly, and glories in the pride of the conquest he has gained. There are few, I think, who, if they will avow the truth, will not admit that at some portion of their lives, they have entertained emotions akin to these.

What the sight of blood may have been supposed to effect in the minds of a gladiator or a Domitian, the touch of her warm tears then produced on me. They thrilled to my heart through every vein, and left the fire of hell behind.

"We last met," I cried, with a stern calmness, " on a fatal day; but do you remember our previous meeting! Do you remember *my* tears, *my* supplications? Do you remember my remorse, my abject submission, my despair, my vows of expiation? —I humbled myself to the dust before you; and I cried, Forgive me, but forgive me, and the rest of my life shall be devoted to atonement! By every possible claim that the most ardent love and the most sincere contrition could imagine, I conjured you to pardon me. And how did you reply?— Immutable, inexorable, you stood like Fate over my future fortune, and you said, 'It shall come to you in darkness and in sorrow; in weeping, wailing, and gnashing of teeth.' You gave me curses for my tears, scorn for my humility, and hatred for my affection. And then my love was turned into bitterness, and I promised that I would be revenged. I ask you whether I have not fulfilled my promise? Haughty destroyer of my peace on earth, of my salvation hereafter, where and what are you now?—I left you then, in the height of your pride, in the strength of your despotism, in the inflexibility of your

vindictiveness. You stood like the destroying angel in my path, flashed the savage
lightnings of your vengeance at my heart, and
hurled me to the ground like a riven tree,
blighted, sapless, blasted! But where and
what are you *now?*—You will not answer!
Beneath the roof of him you loathed, prostrate
at the feet of him you contemned, your self-
debasement is too great for utterance!—Well,
listen then to me. When we met that day,
M———, the vigor of youth was on me; I
was as energetic in mind as in body. Look
on me now—mark this withered arm, this
hollow cheek, this emaciated frame. Think
you, I will ever forgive the author of this
change? Cold-blooded, selfish woman, as obstinate as irresolute—as obstinate in evil as
irresolute in duty! And yet you say you

love me. *You* love *me?* Do you remember
my claims to your affection? Forget you so
soon the misty morn, when blood-stained,
dishevelled, breathing hatred and vengeance,
you stood like a fallen spirit before me, invoked curses on my head, and denounced *me*,
your adorod *now*, as the assassin of your
brother?—Faithless, fickle sister, remember
you not that in boyhood, like a coward and
a fiend, I stabbed him in the *back;* and that,
in manhood, mine was the bullet that sent
him to heaven or to hell?—Ha! ha! ha!
even now I can see his convulsive leap!—
It was his last!"

While I poured forth this devilish rhap-
sody, the unhappy girl, in the intenseness of
her agony, had raised herself in the bed;
and, in this constrained position, remained

glaring on me with eyes that appeared about
to break from their sockets. When I had
concluded, she uttered no sound, but the
rigidity of her muscles was relaxed, and her
head fell on her breast; then, raising it towards heaven, she exclaimed,

" God is just ! Where I have sinned, there
have I been punished. Great is the power of
God!"

Her eyes closed, a ghastly paleness came
over her, and she sank on the bed in a death-
like swoon.

I threw myself upon her body—I stamped
—I foamed—I cursed—I blasphemed. But
why continue this endless picture of revolting
ferocity? She recovered from her trance,
listened, and yielded to my wildly sincere
protestations of contrition; and thus un-

wittingly supplied me with the power of renewing my crimes. Though I felt that mine
might prove the triumph of the Gladiator
who died in receiving the submission of his
enemy, yet I resolved to pursue it.

I assumed unto myself the power of Heaven. I drew an imaginary line, and I said,
" So far will I go, and no farther. Such
has been her offence, and such is the exact
portion of retribution it deserves, and such
shall be inflicted. I will then take her to my
arms, devote my life to her service, and make
her an object of envy to the proudest and to
the happiest."

It was agreed that we should be married as
soon as the necessary preparations could be
arranged, which I volunteered personally to
superintend through all their different de-

partments. I instructed my sister to intrust me even with the selection of my bride's wardrobe.

Eight days passed, during which I was neither attentive nor neglectful, neither affectionate nor repulsive. If I did not woo with all the fervor of passion, I did not exhibit the coldness of indifference.—Whatever she might feel, I gave her no opportunity of declaring by word or look her sense of the alteration in my conduct.

On the ninth day, I was the unseen auditor of a conversation between her and my sister, who was as yet in ignorance of my fiend-like violence on the morning of our interview. They were sitting at a window commanding an uninterrupted view of the magnificent lake beneath, the surface of which was as smooth and unbroken as that of a mirror.

"How lovely is the day," said my sister; "how heavenly! The earth, the sky, the water, all seem to smile. Surely you must sympathize in this jubilee of nature; it ought to reanimate the dead. Dear friend, you *must* learn to surmount this dejection."

She slowly replied, "I fear that it is too deeply radicated ever to be conquered."

"Say not so," rejoined my sister : "if you will not recur to the past, you must be happy—Look to the future :—let us talk of your marriage—the weather is in unison with all joyful things. I wonder what festivity my brother is preparing for us; reserved as he is, I can discover that he is occupied with some

project. Are you not curious to learn what
it is?—I am. If my mind were not engaged
by other interests, I should be very prone to
curiosity. It is a woman's privilege, and her
duty.—Do you not think so?"

The only reply she could obtain was a
melancholy smile.

"I perceive," continued my sister, "that
I must talk for both of us. Come, let us plan
the routine of your domestic life; at what
hour you will rise, when you will go to bed,
the number of your equipages, the extent of
your retinue, the situation of your abode, and
the harmony of your jewels. Emeralds and
diamonds, I think, assort most beautifully;
and yet, there is something exquisitely en-
chanting in the modest pearl. My brother,
you know, is richer than a king; and I need

not tell you that he will devote himself and
his wealth to the promotion of your happiness."

"I hope he will," she said; "and I feel
this desire less for mine than for his own
sake."

"I believe you implicitly, most disinter-
ested of human creatures," cried my sister;
"but why appear to throw a doubt on that
which is indubitable? *Hope?*—You *must*
be happy. But you have not answered my
questions. Tell me, then, where will you reside? My brother's power in this district is
quite despotic; will you then settle here, and
reign the queen of a feudal establishment, or
will you travel for a year or two after your
marriage? Shall we go to Paris, and see the
court of the great king? or to Italy, the land

of romance and literature, of poetry and paint-
ing, of marble palaces and stately ruins? But,
dear sister, you depress *me* at last;—how melancholy you look! and that gloomy robe of
yours so adds to the piteousness of your appearance;—how glad I shall be to see you in
your bridal dress!"

Their conversation ceased, and I left the
place of my concealment with a smile on my
countenance—but not of pleasure.

The tenth, our nuptial day, arrived. My
affianced bride arose, wan and languid, with
an aching heart and a dejected spirit. Her
health had received a fearful blow; paleness
was on her cheek, and melancholy in her dark,
beaming eye. And here, though the recurrence torture me, I feel irresistibly impelled
to dwell for a moment on the extraordinary

loveliness of those singular eyes. Liquid,
mild, and pellucid as the fawn's, yet dark and
penetrating, they could flash with the fire of
love, or, as I too well knew, with the fire of
hate. Sometimes sparkling and playful, more
frequently sedate and reflecting, the individual
they rested upon, felt conscious that he was
under the inspection of one who possessed a
mind which could correctly estimate the qualities of his own. But their most distinguish-
ing feature existed in their peculiar and exquisitely beautiful colour. Were I to say
that they contained a shade which resembled
the dark rich red-brown of the raisin of
Smyrna, the homely nature of my simile
might suggest an idea the most opposite to
my intention; and yet, I know not to what
they could be compared with more accuracy,

though they sometimes reminded me of the auburne of her own bright hair.

How often does the expression of those eyes on that memorable morn recur to me! How often now am I nearly maddened by the re-collection of their piteous, plaintive, exqui-sitely pathetic glances! and how often now do I consider with wonder how I could have borne them without relenting! They beamed a melancholy, at once timid, submissive, de-precating, which might have touched the heart of a fiend—but, I was that worse thing —a bad man, intent on evil. And who, since the days of the first sinner, " that for an apple damned mankind," has ever been known vo-luntarily to turn from the commission of a contemplated and cherished iniquity ?—.

We were at breakfast when her bridal dress

was brought into the room. It was composed entirely of *black* crape. Under the first impulse of surprise, she addressed to me a look of inquiring wonder; but marking the expression of my eye, she read that this strange ill-omened apparel originated in no error of a menial, but in the pre-conceived determination of wilful malevolence.

" Surely," I cried, in reply to her interrogative glance, " such nuptial rites as ours cannot be solemnized according to common forms. *We* do not wed under common circumstances. Even in the feudal days of Catholicism and barbarity, when the curb of morality lay loosely on mankind, interdicts have been issued, kingdoms accursed, and churches desecrated, on account of far less unholy marriages. Think not, then, that in

these times of purer faith and conduct, I will
consent that we shall be united without ex-
hibiting at least some external mark of sorrow
and penitence. I cannot consider myself su-
perstitious, but were I to omit this trifling
expiation, I should apprehend some awful
catastrophe to our impious and unnatural
union."

While I spoke, the mortal paleness of her
cheek increased to a fearful degree; but she
made no reply, and submissively taking the
robe from my hand, withdrew to her chamber.

Shortly afterwards she descended, clothed
in her funereal habiliments. I had passed the
interim in arraying myself in garments of a
similar hue, and I now joined her with an
appearance and air as sombre as her own.
The tramp of horses was heard. I drew her

to the window; and as she gazed on the objects beneath, I felt her hand tremble in my grasp.

She looked indeed on no festival array; no glittering retinue, no splendid equipages, no mirthful faces, no marks were there, to tell that one of the richest commoners of England was about to celebrate his union with one of her fairest daughters. And yet, she looked upon our bridal pageant—two carriages covered externally, and internally, with crape; each of them drawn by six stately horses, black—black as my own heart, in their hue. On their heads they bore a profusion of feathers, of the same funereal colour; and the two or three attendant menials were as darkly and gloomily arrayed.

"What think you of our nuptial procession?" I cried: "it is not absurdly gay, but it is congenial to our feelings, and to our relative circumstances."

She seemed as though her heart were breaking. I gazed on her with an intentness that sought to penetrate her soul. She turned on me her lovely eyes, and said with a holy fervor :—

" May God in heaven forgive you for this cruelty!"

My sister sat sobbing violently in a distant corner of the room. Previously she had adopted every means she could imagine to endeavour to divert me from my persecution. She had reasoned, and persuaded; threatened, and intreated; appealed to every feeling in succession—but in vain. She now arose to make a last effort, but reading on my face

the stubbornness of my heart, she returned to
her seat in silent despair.

" You do not," I cried, addressing my intended bride with ironical courtesy, " you do
not disapprove of the arrangements I have
made?"

On *her* cheek was no trace of a tear; *her*
grief was beyond this source of alleviation;
but her dry eye beamed with a divine resignation, as she replied,

" You have only to inflict, and I will endure
in silence, if not in patience."

A painful smile of assumed incredulity was
my only rejoinder to this most touching proof
of unequalled meekness and charity—of all
that is beautiful in the human heart.

We descended; and I supported her into
the first carriage. The attendant menials

slowly arranged themselves; we began to advance at the solemn and stately pace of a funereal procession; and we were left alone in that dark prison to our own dark thoughts.

I had taken my seat opposite to her; and resolutely fixed my eyes upon her face with the unsteady desperation of a man, consciously sinning. For a moment, she intently examined my countenance; and then turned away with a mingled expression of hopelessness and pity. I began to feel the full iniquity of my demoniac conduct.

She spoke not; and oppressed, and humbled by my strong sense of my own unworthiness, I could not force my parched lips to utter an articulate sound. A word, perhaps, might have diminished the intensity of my agony; but, fettered, in that horrid silence,

face to face, with my innocent victim, I feel and
hope, that the oppressor must have suffered
far more than the oppressed.   Every instant
seemed an eternity; my spirit sank as I gazed
on the exquisite melancholy of her infinitely
beautiful countenance, and I knew not where
to turn to hide me from the consciousness of
my baseness.   I feared to meet her eye; yet,
I was compelled to confront her: and I felt
so keenly the ignominy of the tyranny I was
acting, that I writhed beneath an agony of
shame.   How I then pined to escape from
the thraldom of that accursed vehicle, and ex-
ecrated myself, and the vindictiveness which
had brought me there, God, and my own
heart, alone can tell!

And yet, even then, in that very moment,
I could not resolve to forego the task which I

had imposed on myself. I would have given worlds to have possessed the power of re-treating; but I was far beyond the efforts of self-control. I seemed to myself as though impelled by some dark agency independent of my will; and it would have been more feasible to have arrested in mid-air a rock hurled from the loftiest battlement, than to have diverted me from my fatal course.

We reached the village church, and, with a feeling of almost delirious exultation, I sprang from the accursed confinement. My sister, who had followed us in the other car-riage, joined with me in assisting her to alight; and, affectionately supporting her, gently drew her towards the entrance. As they thus ad-vanced, with their arms interlaced, strange and striking was the contrast between the

funereal apparel of the one, and the white,
flowing bridal robe of the other; for neither
by intreaty nor threat could I induce my conscientious sister to descend to a co-operation
in this unholy mockery. Even in that moment, which of the two I loved the more, I
did not doubt; but, such was the blindness
of my distempered mind, that my *sister* was
then the one who excited my principal interest
and pity.

A more strange, and yet more impressive
contrast awaited us; perhaps a more *startling*
one can scarcely be imagined, than that which
presented itself as we left the open day, the
green and gay fields, and the fragrant earth
and air, and stepped into the little church.
Without, all was natural gaiety and life;
within, were assembled all the artificial means

of inspiring the mind with pain and apprehension. The walls, pews, ceiling, and floor,
were covered with black crape; there was not
a portion of the interior which revealed the
material of which it was composed: wherever
the eye turned, it rested on nought but continued blackness. Numerous flambeaux, im-
pregnated with a sickly perfume, were scattered about; the smoke of which ascended
in white heavy clouds to the roof, and then
tumbled again to earth, oppressing the senses,
and increasing the uncertainty of the gloomy
delusion. The windows, too, had all been
carefully covered with hangings of the same
lugubrious hue; but in some parts, the bright
beams of the broad sun faintly penetrating
the insufficient veil, painfully intermingled
with the strange glare of the red light of the

torches. On either side of the altar, and elevated to the level of its summit, by supporters
appareled in all the trappings of the grave,
were two coffins; the one bearing my name,
the other, her own: blank spaces being reserved for the introduction of the age of the
deceased, and the date of the death.

The general effect of the whole contrivance
was such as might have excited uneasiness and
displeasure in the minds of the most resolute;
but, in the timid and apprehensive, unmitigated
awe and terror. And this was the scene I had
prepared for the celebration of my marriage.

But *she* did not quail; she looked around
her with an unwavering glance, and the agitation of her features gradually subsided into
the quietude of despair—of that despair which
neither hopes nor fears. Once she turned

upon me her deep liquid eyes, with an expression more piteous than reproachful, then
raising them to Heaven, appeared to be absorbed in prayer. She seemed to have been
penetrated by a deep sense of my unworthiness, and to have lost in this conviction both
the power and the desire of combating with
her grief.

Advancing to the altar, she resolutely read
the inscriptions on the two coffins. Touching gently with her fore-finger the one which
described her own name, she said slowly and
emphatically, and so calmly that I almost
thought a smile rested for an instant on her
pallid features,

" You will soon have to supply the omissions
in this brief history of my career; perchance

I may require this duty of you within *seven* days."

Perhaps of all passions, cruelty is that which is most strengthened by indulgence; the more it attains, the more it desires. The man who has once tasted it, is inspired with an insatiate thirst; and the last cup of blood he has drained to the dregs, but renders its successor more enticing. Unlike other vices that decay with the strength of the body which engendered them, this flourishes in an inverse ratio, and only departs with the breath of its possessor, unless some rare shock intervene to recall him to a consciousness of his guilt. Instigated by the natural bent of their dispositions, the Mariuses, the Syllas, the Domitians, the Maximins, began their career of slaughter; but they continued it long after the original impulse must have ceased, in the mere love of the stimulus to which they had been accustomed.

These were the reflections of my after life: at the time of the occurrence of the actions which gave rise to them, I was little capable of analyzing the emotions which maddened me.

"You suffer," I said, "beneath the indignities which I am practising upon you. You may yet retreat. The snare is laid, the chain is forged, the bond is prepared, but bondage is not yet upon you. There is the altar; yonder waits the patient priest—the heifer is found and arrayed for the slaughter; but your freedom is still your own, and your voice can still prevent the accomplishment of the sacrifice.   Speak!—mine must be a *vo-luntary* victim.   I seek neither to lure nor to force you into the captivity you may regret; through your own weakness alone, and not through my strength, must I possess you.   I wear no mask; I stand before you ho-nestly and overtly with the stamp of hell upon me; and though I may be better, I cannot be *worse* than I appear.   Speak! spontaneously I invest you with the power of discarding me a *second* time;" and I trembled with fear, as in the pride and madness of my heart I wan-tonly provoked this decision of my fate.

"Oh, avail yourself of the liberty which the tyrant has proffered you!" exclaimed my sister with energy.   "Deceive not yourself, dear, suffering angel, with the vain thought that he can still entertain for you one particle of genuine affection. Strive not to attribute this infernal usage to the ebullition of passion, however insane; it is the cold-blooded result of systematized cruelty, and there is no hope, here or hereafter, for the man that can have committed it. Oh, brother, brother! I live to lament the ties that unite us. In the words of the prophet I denounce you: 'Wo unto the wicked, it shall be ill with him; for the reward of his hands shall be given to him!' "

As she thus spoke, with all the elevation and the energy of the inspired writer whose language she adopted, she approached her unfortunate friend, and tenderly and lovingly supporting her, attempted to lead her from the church. But I interposed, in the intention of separating them.

" Touch me not! touch me not, brother!"

she exclaimed, with a startling emphasis, and more startling gesture, " or your hand shall be even as the hand of Jéroboam !"

For a moment, I was disconcerted, nay, arrested, by this impetuous burst of honest passion; and I angrily and threateningly scowled on the enthusiastic girl; though even then, I could not forbear from honoring and revering her for her noble affection and integrity.

But the demon had set his seal upon me; I was his, for ever; and the interposition of an angel might have failed to have turned me from my purposes. The virtues and example of my high-minded sister caused me not even to waver; they fell harmlessly as pointless darts from the iron of my breast. I resolutely approached, and was more firmly renewing

my attempt to separate them, when my intended bride, gently and tenderly extricating
herself from the grasp of her clinging and
reluctant friend, thus impressively addressed
her :—

" Kind, consistent, beloved, and affectionate
being, interest not yourself in the lot of one
who has no longer a stake in this earthly game :
Fate has defined for me my course, and I
must passively fulfil it. Be not too rigid with
your brother; for he, alas, is not the only
sinner; I, too, have committed a sin, and I
will expiate it. Had I once listened to his
contrition, perhaps he would not now have
hardened his heart against my sorrow."

" O reflect, reflect!" cried her agitated
friend; " for your sake, for my sake, dear,

beloved one, do not resign yourself to this bad man !"

" Silence, sister !" I exclaimed, in a thundering voice, and in a paroxysm of insane and fearful passion.

The poor girl bent beneath my fury, and stood tremblingly, tearfully mute, by the side of her still more pallid friend; who with a thousand gentle caresses, affectionately endeavoured to restore her.   Then turning to me, she exclaimed,

" Strange and inscrutable being, you seek to wed me, and yet you woo me *thus!*" and she gazed around her with a look of blended mournfulness and gentle reproach, which was ineffably pathetic.   "But doubt not my determination.   No!" she emphatically cried,

" no! I will *not* retract. I can now adopt
your own words and say, ' I had set my all
upon a cast, and I will stand the hazard of the
die.' I had long deemed you the possessor of
the noblest qualities, of a high and virtuous,
though an impetuous mind; but in discerning
the falsity of my valuation, in learning that he
whom I had almost elevated into a divinity is
but—" she paused, and then added, " an
erring man, I have lost the sole delusion that
rendered existence desirable to me. You have
embittered even the memory of the past; I
can no longer say ' To-morrow do thy worst,
for I have lived to-day.' I possess not even
that support, for I feel that there was no
reality in my imaginings, and that I have
been the shallow victim of my own self-de-
ception. Without a hope, without a fear,

why should I retract? I will not prove apostate to the ardent wish of years; and here I now stand, not in the weakness of abject affection, but in the strength of despair, prepared to die—*your wife;*" and she held forth her hand. I seized it, and pressing it in triumph to my lips, led her to the altar.

The ceremony was concluded. During its celebration she evinced no further emotion, but unresistingly allowed herself to be directed through its various forms in apparent unconsciousness, if not in real apathy.

We emerged from this oppressive and fetid scene of darkness and vapour into the pure air, light, and fragrance of Heaven. The contrast was quite overwhelming; during a few moments my sister and I remained confounded beneath its dazzling influence. But cold, pale, rigid,

and impassive, my unhappy bride exhibited
no more consciousness of external impressions
than the statue she resembled.

I suggested that we should walk to our
home; she assented with the docility of in-
fantine dependence. In the abstraction of her
grief, in the utter prostration of her broken
spirit, she seemed no longer to possess a will
of her own, but to depend for her impulses
on the agency of others. I placed her arm
on mine, she allowed me to caress it; I advanced, she yielded to the movement, and
submissively followed. I grasped her hand,
she returned the pressure; I approached my
lips to her face, and with unconscious defer-
ence she turned her pale cheek to receive the
kiss I bestowed. Not when she lay before
me in suspended animation was she less the

mistress of her reason than at this moment.
As I contemplated this perfect personification
of loveliness congealed by sorrow into a mere
mockery of reason, my demoniac resolution
began to fail me; but the rejection—the
accursed rejection recurred to my mind. Beneath its blighting influence, like the Pharaoh
of old, again my heart was hardened, and I
swore that she should drain the cup of retribution, even to the dregs.

During these reflections we had reached
the summit of the hill we had been ascending.
A portion of the wood close to, and immediately before us, had recently been felled, and
in the space thus opened, appeared a hand-
some marble structure. The eyes of my sister
expressed undisguised surprise and uneasiness,
but the countenance of my bride still retained

its painful rigidity. We advanced still nearer,
and an inscription then became visible, to
which in stern silence I motioned the attention of my wife. Aroused by my action, by
the singularity of the scene, perhaps by a
prophetic apprehension, with a faltering step,
and a cheek alarmed into life, as though
under the influence of some infernal fascina-
tion, she slowly obeyed the lingering motion
of my finger, and tracked it until she reached
the tomb, and read

ERECTED IN ETERNAL RECORD OF THE
CRIME, ON THE SCENE OF ITS PERPETRA-
TION, TO THE MEMORY OF THE DEAD; BY
HIM WHO COMMITTED THE MURDER, AND
THEN MARRIED THE SISTER OF THE MUR-
DERED.

As though a bolt from Heaven had pierced her heart, she was hurled to the earth with the weight and lifelessness of a stone.

We bore her to our home. During six days she lingered in incessant delirium on the verge of eternity. I dare not describe her ravings, her denunciations, or her prayers. Even now, were I minutely to recall those cursed hours of hellish torture, I could *think* myself into a frenzy equal to her own.

On the morn of the seventh day, she gave symptoms of returning consciousness; before noon, she awakened into life. She gazed around her with intentness; her eyes alighted on my sister and on myself, and she testified her recognition with a melancholy but serene smile. Her attention was then arrested by the sound of the bell of the village-church tolling to announce the commencement of the service.

" It is the Sabbath," she cried; "a day of peace and thanksgiving, and a fitting day for our re-union. My husband, my sister, give me your hands."

We complied, and she pressed them tenderly; her touch was as cold as thawing ice. The expression of her eye, though calm, was painfully plaintive; and her feeble yet still eminently musical voice thrilled through our hearts as she continued:

" In this last, awful moment, I recur to my past life; and, save the one fatal act which I am now expiating, I trust that I have not much to lament. Were I doomed to retrace the deluding scene which I am about to quit, in one only respect would I

o

seek to depart from the course which I have
pursued; I would more frequently devote
my thoughts to a communion with my Creator. The habit of prayer insensibly elevates
the mind, and weakens the force of its worldly
affections. 'Religion is the only thing found
on earth which, like the bee, draws from the
bitter and the sweet the same honied juice;
and, though many ways have been devised
for man to govern his nature, there is but
this one principle which can ever raise him
above it.' I now feel with gratitude to
Heaven, that I have not neglected this consolation; but I have not cultivated it to the
extent of my power."

"You are an angel!" gasped my sobbing
sister;—but *I* had neither voice nor tears.

"Be comforted, dear girl," exclaimed my

unhappy bride, tenderly drawing toward her her affectionate friend, until their lips met. Then, giving her one feeble but long and passionate embrace, she resumed her discourse with more than her previous serenity.

" I do not ask you *not* to lament my loss, for I know that you possess not the power of complying with this demand; but I implore you to repress your feelings in this moment, and conceal from me the grief which I cannot alleviate. Death is upon me; and I feel, and see, and judge with an unwonted perception, as though I were imbued with the spirit of prophecy. Do not, then, I pray, disturb this holy composure, nor again reduce me to the endurance of emotions which partake of the follies and vanities of the world. For your sake, my friend—my husband," she continued, addressing herself to me, " I could wish to have been spared a little longer, to have devoted myself to the restoration of your peace of mind ;—but God's will be done ! To you and to your love, my sister, I now intrust him ; and the last supplication of your dying friend is, that you will devote every affection— every energy, to the mitigation of his anguish. Hear me again declare that I feel that I have wronged him.—Had I listened to him in his agony, this retribution had not befallen us both ; but, in the intemperance of my passion, I rejected his contrition, and the evil that has ensued has alighted, I hope—oh, how I hope !—most heavily on the head of her who was the source of it !"

She paused for a moment, and then continued :

" Hear that village bell : how many vain associations it suggests ! But though I cannot regard the past without an emotion, I am already above its influence. How lovely is the day!—Open the casement, dear sister, and let me breathe the pure air of heaven. Now move me into the sun ; I long to feel its glorious beams play once more upon these icy limbs ! "

We did as she directed ; and she closed her eyes, and lay for a few moments silently inhaling the gentle balmy breeze that floated over her pale face. She threw back her hair, and exposed her brow and temples to its refreshing influence. Again she spoke :

" Earth is fair, and many are the dear delights which it contains ; but this which I now enjoy is the highest and purest of them all. Often have I stood beneath the blue sky, and, on the lake, or on the hill, revelled in the possession of this best blessing ; but never knew I until this moment the extent of the bliss it could confer !—And now, my beloved sister, you can yet farther sooth the bitterness of this parting hour. I could wish before I die to be once more under the exalting influence of music : beneath its inspirations, I might better sustain the pang of separation ; and I feel that I need its divine power to raise me above the fascinations which still enthral me, and its buoyant wings to pilot my soul to Heaven. Embrace me then again, dear friend ;—and now I entreat you to comply with my request. Descend, and play to me that beauteous hymn to the Virgin, *Maria santissima, madre amata,* which I so loved in the days of my happiness."

Oh, God! how did I survive that moment? —Had this angel victim of my accursed ferocity striven, in the deadliness of revenge, to stab me to the soul, she could have devised no wiser mode than this simple allusion to the hour of our first meeting. But groan, word, nor look betrayed the agony that was consuming me; though any crime but mine might have been expiated by what I then endured.

After a last and passionate embrace, with a long, lingering look and a breaking heart, my poor sister left the room; and soon the magnificent peals of the organ filled and thrilled through the house. The face of my

bride became illuminated with a celestial expression, and the agency of Heaven was
visibly upon her. She grasped my hand
with a fervent pressure, and, closing her eyes,
abandoned herself to her divine aspirations.
As the melody proceeded, her hold relaxed,
and without a sigh, a look, the shadow of
a manifestation, the pure spirit quitted its
mortal tenement, and I sustained the arm of
the dead.

———

Fifty years have passed since that day; one
half of them in the indulgence of every ruthless and desperate passion. I deemed existence an injury; I thought myself aggrieved
in having been created; and I felt evil towards all my race. In the profligate court
of Charles, and afterwards in that of Louis,

I found an ample field for my misanthropic
impulses.   Like Ishmael, " my hand was
against every man, and every man's hand
against me."   And yet I prospered in the
world, and earned in it those distinctions of
name and renown which others only obtain
through the exertions of wilful and systematized ambition.   At the head of armies,
in the strife_of courts, in the dangerous in-
trigues of internal politics, in foreign diplo-
macy, in private faction, or in popular tumult,
success invariably attended me.   During this
long career, I was the envied of the many;
and even now, I could direct universal attention to my obscurity, by revealing the
designation under which I drew upon myself
the eyes of Europe.   But neither wealth,
power, nor homage softened the agony of my

remorse; within me was the worm that never dieth.

As I advanced in life, the fiery restlessness, which had hitherto involuntarily propelled me into energetic exertion, forsook me; and the last five and twenty years of my guilty existence have been past, I hope, less erringly than the two first. In solitude and in penitence, in prayer and self-imposed privation, have I striven to subdue the strong wickedness of my heart; but *hæret lateri lethalis arundo*, it goads me night and day, and an ocean of tears could not wash out the memory of the one great crime of my bad life. For ever, and ever, the words of Adoni-bezek recur to me:—" As I have done, so God hath requited me."

No human effort or power can restore me

to tranquillity. Since the hour of her death, the curse of Heaven has been on me and mine; my sisters have died childless, and I live the last of my race. In the morning I wish for the evening, and in the night I wish for the day. The heaven above me is as brass, and the earth beneath me is as iron. Above, below man's wo and joy, I prowl over the face of the land alone amongst millions: an alien to the common passions of my race, I can neither weep with the mourner, nor smile with the happy.—And yet, I fear to die! Existence is my bane, the future is my dread; I loathe what is, but I tremble at what is to be. —May this expiate—May the Almighty be merciful to a wretch who cannot forgive himself!

I do not hope that this gloomy career of

crime and misery can interest, but it may instruct. Though I cannot bequeath a moral legacy as striking as that of the Moorish king, I will yet strive to contribute my mite, though a posthumous one, to the welfare of mankind. I have perpetrated and seen so much evil, have so writhed beneath the horrors of remorse, that I would willingly make any exertion to save a fellow-creature from its stings. I shall not then deem this painful record to have been written in vain, if my example and fate serve but to turn one sinner to repentance, or to impress on the mind of one waverer the conviction that

VIRTUE IS THE ONLY SOURCE OF HAPPINESS.

NOTES.

Page 37, line 3.

Before the rude Thessalian had caused the young and the lovely to be superseded by the staid matron of fifty.

The office of priestess in the Temple of Apollo at Delphi was for many years fulfilled by a youthful and beautiful virgin; but in consequence of a Thessalian of the name of Echecrates having assaulted one of them, it was decreed that for the future none but women above the age of fifty, and correspondingly ugly, should undertake the sacred office.

Page 67, line 1.

I could be inspired with that of Mezentius.

A tyrant of Italy, who used to tie the living to the

dead, and leave them without food to perish in this fearful company.

Page 140, line 11.

Like Regulus in his murderous cask.

Among other tortures inflicted on Regulus, after he was taken by the Carthaginians, was that of confining him in a barrel lined with iron spikes, in which he was rolled until he expired in infinite agony.

Page 160, line 2.

The triumph of the Gladiator, who died in receiving the submission of his enemy.

An Athenian, of the name of Arrichion, who, prostrate on the ground, and half suffocated in the grasp of his enemy with a dying effort, seized him by the foot, and broke one of his toes. The anguish of the fracture caused him to cry for quarter, in the very moment that Arrichion himself expired. But he had lived to be victor, and the judges awarded that his body should be crowned.

Page 184, line 2.

Or your hand shall be even as the hand of Jeroboam.

" And it came to pass, when King Jeroboam heard the saying of the man of God, which had cried against the altar in Bethel, that he put forth his hand from the altar, saying, Lay hold on him. And his hand which he put forth against him dried up, so that he could not put it in again."—1 *Kings*, chap. xiii.

Page 202, line 16.

As I have done, so God hath requited me.

" But Adoni-bezek fled, and they pursued after him, and caught him, and cut off his thumbs and his great toes.

" And Adoni-bezek said, Three score and ten kings having their thumbs and their great toes cut off, gathered their meat under my table: as I have done, so God hath requited me !"—*The Book of Judges*, chap. i.

Page 204, line 2.

Though I cannot bequeath a moral legacy as striking as that of the Moorish king.

Abderame, or Abdalrahman the third, the great Caliph of Cordova, who left in his own hand this estimate of the value of earthly grandeur and felicity:— " Fifty years have I reigned. Riches, honors, pleasures, I have enjoyed them all—exhausted them all. The kings, my rivals, fear me, and envy me, yet esteem me. All that men desire has been lavished on me by heaven. In this long space of apparent felicity I have calculated the number of days in which I have been really happy; they amount to *fourteen.* Mortals, learn how to appreciate greatness, the world, and life."

LONDON:
PRINTED BY W. WILCOCKSON, WHITEFRIARS.

trism

prea
g est-
ry:-
pher-
: a.
rd
&
it;
ti